WRITING VIVID SETTINGS

CW00894266

Cover art and design by Erica Sy~~~~~~
Scimitar Press (February 2015 Paperback Edition)
St. Leonards

WRITING VIVID SETTINGS

Rayne Hall

CONTENTS

INTRODUCTION

Do you want your readers to feel like they're really there—in the place where the story happens?

By creating vivid settings, you can bring this about. Your readers will breathe the cool mountain air, feel the icy wind sting their cheeks, and sink their toes into the moist sand.

Some authors create sumptuous descriptions for the readers to savour like a rich banquet, others serve theirs like a salad, lean and crisp. Whichever style you choose, you must craft your setting descriptions so they increase the appetite for the story.

I love settings the way other people love chocolate. But my early descriptions were sticky gunk, calorie-laden with little flavour. Long-winded and dull, they spread over many paragraphs and mired down the action. Unsurprisingly, readers skipped them. Now I craft setting descriptions where every sentence melts in the mouth like a luxury chocolate truffle.

Whether you want to enrich stark prose with atmospheric detail, add vibrancy to a dull piece or curb waffling descriptions, this guide can help. Learn how to make your settings intense, realistic, and intriguing.

Most chapters show tricks you can apply to every scene. Some give suggestions for specific situations, such as night scenes, romance, scary moments, and fights.

Try the techniques and add them to your toolkit. Then decide which tool to use for which scene, and how. I'm teaching the craft, but the choice of how to apply it is your art. Don't rely on a single tool, because any technique becomes tedious if overused. Interpret my techniques creatively. When you infuse them with your own taste and personality, you create your unique author voice.

To get the most from this guide, you need to have mastered the basics of the writer's craft. It doesn't teach you how to plot a story or construct a scene, but it shows you how to enhance them with vivid settings.

If you like, you can use this book as a self-study class, approaching each chapter as a lesson and completing the assignments at the end of each session.

To avoid the clunky 'he or she does this with her or him', I use sometimes the male pronoun and sometimes the female. Everything I write in this book applies to either gender. I'm writing in British English, so my grammar, punctuation, spellings and word choices may look odd if you're used to American.

Now let's bring your story settings to life.

Rayne Hall

CHAPTER 1: SMELLS FOR REALISM

Here's a powerful technique for immersing readers into your story: use the sense of smell.

Of all the senses, smell has the strongest psychological effect. The mere mention of a smell evokes memories and triggers associations in the reader's subconscious.

Mention a smell, and the scene comes to life. Mention two or three, and the reader is pulled into the scene as if it were real. A single sentence about smells can reveal more about a place than several paragraphs of visual descriptions. This is useful if you aim to keep your descriptions short.

For example, the hero enters a home for old people. *The place smelled of boiled cabbage, urine and disinfectant.* These nine words are enough to convey what kind of old people's home this is, and it creates a strong image in the reader's mind.

Or try these:
The room smelled of pizza, beer and unwashed socks.
The room smelled of beeswax, joss sticks and patchouli.
The corridor smelled of mould and leaking sewage.
The kitchen smelled of coffee, cinnamon and freshly baked bread.
The kitchen smelled of burnt milk, overripe pears and bleach.
The garden smelled of lilacs and freshly mown grass.
The cell smelled of blood, urine and rotting straw.

HOW AND WHERE TO USE THIS TECHNIQUE

The best place to insert a sentence about smells is immediately after the point-of-view (PoV) character has arrived at a new location.
That's when humans are most aware of smells, so it feels right if you mention them.

Smells trigger emotions. If you want your reader to feel positive about the place, use pleasant scents. To make the reader recoil, mention nasty odours.

Also, consider the genre. Thriller and horror readers appreciate being taken to places where odours are as foul as the villain's deeds, but romance readers want a pleasant experience, so treat them to lovely scents.

If you like, you can use this technique in almost every scene. To keep it fresh, vary the sentence structure and the wording. Here are some suggestions:

The place reeked/stank of XX and YY.
The odours of XX and YY mingled with the smells of CCC and DDD.
Her nostrils detected a whiff of XX beneath the smells of YY and CCC.
The smell of XX warred with the stronger odour of YY.
The air was rich with the scents of XX and YY.
The smell of XX failed to mask the stench of YY.
The stench of XX hit him first, followed by the odour of YY.
Beneath the scent of XX lay the more ominous odours of YY and CCC.
The scents of XX and YY greeted her.
The smells of XX and YY made his mouth water.
He braced himself against the stink of XX and YY.

PROFESSIONAL EXAMPLES

These examples show how authors have used this technique in their fiction.

The room smelled like stale smoke and Italian salad dressing. (Michael Connelly: *The Poet*)

I took a couple of deep breaths, smelled rain, diesel and the pungent dead-fish-and-salt stench off the river. (Devon Monk: *Magic to the Bone*)

The place smelt of damp and decay. (Jonathan Stroud: *The Amulet of Samarkand*)

A rare south wind had brought the smell of Tyre to last night's landfall: cinnamon and pepper in the cedar-laced pine smoke, sharp young wine and close-packed sweating humanity, smoldering hemp and horse piss. (Mathew Woodring Stover: *Iron Dawn*)

The smell hit her first: rotting flesh, ancient blood. (Kristine Kathryn Rusch: *Sins of the Blood*)

The air held the warm odours of honey and earth, of pine resin and goat sweat, mingled with the scents of frying oil and spice. (Rayne Hall: *Storm Dancer*)

Its air was stagnant, smelling of corner must, discarded tires, and jugs of used motor oil. (Janet Evanovich: *One for the Money*)

The cold air reeked of cabbages and sweat. (Jason Goodwin: *The Snakestone*)

The air simmered with the reek of garlic and hair pomade (Lindsay Davis: *The Silver Pigs*)

MISTAKES TO AVOID

If the first sentence in every scene is a list of three smells, it becomes predictable and boring. Make it less obvious by varying the wording, the sentence structure and the placement.

Don't overdo the bad smells, or the reader may feel such revulsion that she doesn't want to read on.

ASSIGNMENTS

1. Whatever story you're working on right now, whatever scene you're writing, think of two or more smells that characterise the place. Write a sentence about them, and insert it near the beginning of the scene.

2. When you go somewhere today—to the supermarket, the dentist or the church—pay attention to the smells of the place. Write them down. If you do this for a different place every day, you'll soon have a reference—a Setting Descriptions Bank—you can draw on for future stories.

CHAPTER 2: SOUNDS FOR EXCITEMENT

A sentence describing noises creates a strong atmosphere. At the same time, it rouses the reader's excitement.

You can use two types of sounds: background noises and action noises.

BACKGROUND NOISES

Sounds which are unrelated to the action but characterise the place are perfect for creating atmosphere. You can combine several sounds in a single sentence.

An empty beer can clattered along the pavement.
Keyboards clacked, papers rustled and printers whirred.
Upstairs, a toilet flushed and water gurgled down the drainpipe.
Thunder rumbled in the distance.
Washing machines clicked and sloshed, driers rumbled and coins thunked.
Motors whined, and tyres screeched on the tarmac.
Hooves clattered on the cobblestones below.
The train accelerated with a low growl that gradually rose to a high whine.
Thunder roared, and raindrops hammered against the glass.
The fire in the grate crackled.

When and How To Use Background Noises

You can insert a sentence about background noises in any part of the scene where it makes sense.
It works especially well in these situations:
- The PoV character is waiting (for her job interview, her rescue or her execution).
- A character pauses or delays replying. A sentence like this implies the pause and is more interesting than, *He paused* or, *She hesitated.*

- To emphasise an exciting moment.
- To further raise the suspense in a suspenseful situation, insert a sentence about background noises the moment the reader holds her breath.
- When the setting is dark (for example, at night) sprinkle sounds throughout the scene.

ACTION SOUNDS

Whenever characters do something—walk, work, fight, rest—they do it in a specific space, and their actions interact with their environment. This creates a link between the action and the setting. Emphasise this link, especially if you want the reader to become immersed in the story. The best way to do this is by describing the sounds arising from the characters' interaction with the environment.

When and How to Use Action Sounds

This technique works best for fast-paced, action-rich scenes. It gives the reader a sense of the environment without slowing the pace of the action.

You can add the sound to the sentence containing the action *(He marched out, banging the door behind him)*, or you can create a short separate sentence just for the sound *(The door banged behind him.)*

The door screeched on its hinges.
I sank into the armchair. The seat squealed under my weight.
Stairs creaked under her steps.
Gravel crunched under his feet.
My wheeled suitcase rattled across cracked paving-slabs and patched tarmac.

PROFESSIONAL EXAMPLES

She heard him walk above her somewhere. The heavy click of his heels on the creaky wood floors. The jingle of his keys. Then there was silence. (Jilliane Hoffman: *Pretty Little Things*)

Above her, the security system buzzed, then the elevator whirred and banged. (Kristine Kathryn Rusch: *Sins of the Blood*)

An empty coke can rattled across the concrete, a crisp wrapper rustled along the track, and somewhere in the distance, a motor whined. (Rayne Hall: *The Devil You Know*)

The creek hummed and churned, birds chirped. (Chelsea Cain: *Sweetheart*)

Our footsteps rang fast and sharp on the ancient stone floor. (Lindsey Davis: *The Silver Pigs*)

She thumbed a switch and the doors closed with a hiss and a thump. (Neil Gaiman: *American Gods*)

The Horseshoe reverberates with noise. There are DOs yelling to each other or into the mikes at their shoulders; doors ringing as they are slammed and locked; drunks drying out to friends they've hallucinated into existence. And then there is the bass line: the steady squelch of a working inmate's shoes on the floor as eh mops; the hum of an air-exchange fan; the Christmas jingle of chains as a line of men are shuffled down the hallway. (Jodi Picoult: *Vanishing Acts*)

MISTAKES TO AVOID

Don't just list the noises *(There were sounds of cars and birds.)* Instead, use verbs to bring the sounds to life: *(Cars hummed and birds twittered.)*

ASSIGNMENTS

1. Consider the scene you're writing or revising now. What background noises could there be in the place? Make a list. Combine three of them in a sentence. Insert the sentence into your scene, choosing a moment where the character is waiting for something or has time to listen to the environment.

2. What are the characters doing in the scene you're working on? What noises do their movements create on the floor, or with the furniture or doors?

3. Walk in the street, sit in a coffee shop or pay attention as you travel to work: what noises do you hear? Write them down and add them to your collection of setting descriptions.

CHAPTER 3: LIGHT FOR ATMOSPHERE

To convey the atmosphere of a place, insert a sentence about where the light comes from, its colour and quality.

By phrasing this sentence creatively, you can evoke any kind of atmosphere you want: creepy, gritty, romantic, optimistic, depressed, aggressive, gentle, dire.

HOW AND WHERE TO USE THIS TECHNIQUE

Ask yourself: where does the light in this place come from? Sunlight, candles, lantern, torch, glass wall, bare light bulb, neon strip lights, windows, campfire, ceiling lamp, embroidered table lamp, car headlights? What's its quality? Harsh, gentle, muted, cheery, sparse, intense, bright? What's its colour? Yellow, orange, white?

What does the light do? Instead of something bland, like, *illuminated the room*, choose a creative verb. Does it paint certain patterns? If yes, what kind, and where? Does it reveal, slam, spear, brush, stroke or pierce something? Does it peek, flicker, glow, glare?

If light comes from the window, consider constructing a sentence on this basis:

Cold/cool/bright/warm/white/yellow/golden/pearly/silvery/harsh/mild/gentle/soft   *light fell/dropped/poured/spilled/peeked/trickled/speared/shot/glinted/spread/streaked/burst through the window(s).*

You can create endless variations on that. I'm sure one of them will suit your indoor scene.

You can also add:
... and painted/drew/threw/sent/slammed/spattered [adjective & noun describing shapes] on the [adjective & noun describing items of furniture or parts of the room].

Examples:

Harsh light shot through the windows and painted sharp rectangles on the tiled floor.
Golden light trickled through the window and painted soft rectangles on the lush carpet.

When writing outdoor scenes, describe if something glints, gleams or sparkles in the light. The quality of the light differs at different times of the day. In the morning, the light tends to be cool and clear, showing everything in bright colours with crisp outlines. Around noon and early afternoon, the light is intense and harsh, with very short shadows, and everything looks washed-out and pale. In the late afternoon, the light becomes softer, warmer, dipping everything in a golden glow, and the shadows lengthen. Sunset brings magnificent colour effects. (Note: these effects can vary depending on where in the world the story takes place.)

Shadows are great, too, especially if you want to create suspense, foreboding or uncertainty. In outdoors scenes, you can also use them to indicate the time of the day. Do they flicker, lengthen, shorten, shrink, reach, spread, dance?

The sentence about light often works best near the beginning of the scene, though you can also use it later, especially if the light changes (shadows grow longer, candle flame dies).

One sentence is usually enough, but if you aim for a lush descriptive writing style, you can write a whole paragraph.

PROFESSIONAL EXAMPLES

Many bestselling authors rely on this technique for creating atmosphere.

The Morelli garage hunkered detached and snubbed at the edge of their lot. It was a sorry affair, lit by a single shaft of light filtering through a grime-coated window. (Janet Evanovich: *One For The Money.*)

The four narrow windows, set high in the walls, were hardly larger than embrasures, and the dust-filmed panes of glass permitted only weak, chalky light to enter. Even brightened by a pair of lamps, the big room held on tenaciously to its shadows, unwilling to be completely disrobed. The flickering amber light from the lamps revealed damp stone walls and a hulking, coal-fired furnace that was cold and unused on this fine, warm May afternoon. (Dean Koontz: *The Mask*)

Behind them the sun rose over the horizon. Every slight rise in the desert was gilded, every tiny depression a pool of black ink. As they rode, their shadows flickered far out in front as if in a futile attempt to outrun them. (Harry Sidebottom: *King of Kings*)

A sliver of soft sunlight pierced a crack in the silk drapes. (Jeff Abbot: *Panic*)

Morning light cut through the crack in the curtains and slashed its mark across the bleached pine floor. He watched particles of dust floating lazily in the light near the sliding glass door. (Michael Connelly: *The Black Echo*)

The sand shifted in the waning light and dust billowed up in a shimmering haze (Michelle Moran: *Nefertiti*)

The first grudging rays flickered in the eastern sky. A halo of light slowly emerged over the Docklands horizon. (Jonathan Stroud: *The Amulet of Samarkand*)

Incongruously, there were more fishermen now, hooded and wrapped against the cold, small green lights alongside them puncturing the night. Car headlights flickering in the waters of the canal. (John Harvey: *Darkness & Light*)

The apartment was a well of shadows, oil-black and pooled deep. Faint ash-gray light outlined the windows but provided no illumination to the room (Dean Koontz: *The Bad Place*)

I roll up my blinds and the light floats in. (Vikram Seth, *An Equal Music*)

White oak floors gleamed like polished glass. Sunlight streamed in through floor-to-ceiling windows. (Tess Gerritsen: The Apprentice)

The sun gleaming upon that brilliant patch of clear, restful colour, with the dark glow of the bare desert around it, made it shine like the purest emerald in a setting of burnished copper. (Arthur Conan Doyle: *The Tragedy of the Korosko*)

MISTAKES TO AVOID

If you use this technique in every scene, make sure you describe different light effects and vary the sentence structure. If the sun glints off armour in one scene, the campfire glints off armour in the second and torchlight does the same in the third, it becomes tedious.

ASSIGNMENTS

1. For the scene you're currently working on, decide the time of the day, the source(s) of the light, and the kind of atmosphere you want to create. Craft one sentence about the light, and insert it into the scene.

2. Take your notebook with you. When you have a moment to spare—in the supermarket, at the bus stop, in the pub, on the beach—observe the colour and quality of light, and write it in your notebook. If you're not going anywhere, you can simply look out of your window and describe a light effect. Collect light observations for as many places as possible. Save them in a file for future use—your Setting Descriptions Bank.

CHAPTER 4: COLOUR FOR MOOD

When describing colours, don't stick to boring *red, white* and *green*. Instead, have fun and come up with creative phrases. Choose phrases which convey a mood and place hints in the reader's subconscious.

If you describe a street scene in autumn, with leaves dotting the pavements, don't just say that the leaves are yellow. Instead, say that they're *yellow like splatters of vomit* or *yellow like scattered gold coins*. Both evoke a similar vision, but a vastly different mood.

HOW AND WHERE TO USE THIS TECHNIQUE

You can apply this technique throughout your story, whenever and as much as you like.
You may want to use the following constructs:

- 'noun-[name of colour]' (for example: chocolate-brown, turd-brown, rosehip-red, spinach-green, dandelion-yellow)

- 'the colour of [adjective plus noun]' (the colour of a stagnant pond, the colour of washed-out jeans)

- '[noun]-coloured' (vomit-coloured, ketchup-coloured)

- 'as [name of colour] as [adjective plus noun]' (as white as a freshly-laundered bed sheet, as red as tomato sauce)

Most descriptions will involve a simile (comparing the colour to a similar-coloured object). Try to use similes which come natural to your PoV character. Compare the colour of the new item with something from your PoV's range of experience.

For example, something is white. If your PoV is a chef, she'll think *as white as wheat flour*, a mason thinks *plaster-white* and secretary *as white as printer-paper*, while for a housekeeper the same colour may be *as white as a freshly starched linen sheet.*

Colours can create a sense of danger, foreboding or violence if you describe something as *bruise-coloured, the colour of bleached bones* or *the colour of a fresh wound.*

Colours can evoke periods or contexts:

the green of a 1950s kidney table
the green of a 1980s bathroom suite
the pink of his grandmother's slippers
the red of the priest's stole at Easter Mass

Even if the readers aren't familiar with the colour trends of bygone periods, even if they've never attended Easter Mass, and have never seen the PoV's grandmother's slippers, they'll get a strong message about the colour and what it represents to the character.

The exact colour often matters less than the mood it evokes. For example, *the colour of icing on an oversweet cake* is not very specific, but it reveals a lot about the PoV's attitude.

PROFESSIONAL EXAMPLES

Walls were painted bone-white. (Lisa Gardner: *The Killing Hour*)

The bare-limbed trees were ash-coloured, as if they had been severely scorched by a long-extinguished fire (Dean Kootz: *Darkfall*)

A candelabra of twisted iron spikes burned with candles the shade of tomato soup, in the middle of the glass dining table. (Tanith Lee: *When the Lights Go Out*)

The sky was bruise blue and flesh pink behind a swaddling of pure white cumulus, hinting at the frigid clarity to come. (Michael Faber: *Under the Skin*)

At last, bits of daylight peered through the nicotine-coloured plastic blinds. (Rayne Hall: *Night Train*)

MISTAKES TO AVOID

Don't use clichés to describe colours (*as white as the fallen snow, grass green, pitch black, blood red*). Instead, think of fresh phrases.

ASSIGNMENTS

1. Look around you. Observe the colour of an item, and think of three different creative ways to describe this colour. Add these phrases to your Setting Descriptions Bank.

2. What mood do you want to create for the scene you're currently working on? Describe the colour of something in the setting in a way that evokes that mood.

CHAPTER 5: WEATHER FOR INTENSITY

Here is one of the simplest yet most powerful tools in the writer's toolkit: the weather.

New writers often ignore this tool, but bestselling authors use it a lot to create atmosphere, magnify tension and build intensity.

Using the weather can spice up any scene in any genre. You can choose weather that's typical for the location and the season, or freaky weather. Whether a hot wind sucks all moisture from the place, or a steady downpour soaks everything, a scene with specific weather immediately becomes vivid.

Places look very different in different kinds of weather, which allows you to create interesting, atmospheric descriptions.

Just don't choose nice, normal, non-descriptive weather. 'Nice and normal' makes bland fiction.

Characters perceive the surroundings differently depending on the weather. If your main character (MC) arrives at a holiday destination and it's hot and sunny, she'll probably find the place pleasant. But if rain is pouring by the bucket, or if a chilly mist blocks the view, she'll feel frustrated.

The weather affects the PoV character's (and therefore the reader's) experience. Driving along a country road feels differently if it's baking-oven hot and the tarmac is melting, than if the rain pours faster than her windscreen wipers can clear it away, or if snow covers an ice-slick road. Your MC will feel differently, drive differently, behave differently.

The more extreme the weather is, the more intense the scene becomes. Extreme weather brings out the best or the worst in people. Prolonged bad weather makes people bad-tempered. Heatwaves can make some people tired and other people passionate. Weather conditions can isolate people. Imagine a group of people who can't get out of their hut for two weeks because they're snowed in. They feel trapped by surroundings and act accordingly. Tempers will flare.

HOW AND WHERE TO USE THIS TECHNIQUE

If you have a relatively bland scene that needs livening up, perhaps a transition scene in which not much action happens, then change the weather and see what happens. Your protagonists will suddenly feel and act differently, and everything becomes more interesting.

If you revisit the same place for several scenes in your novel, consider changing the weather each time, perhaps according to the seasons.

During the Black Moment and Climax scenes of your novel, choose extreme weather—a blizzard, a hurricane, a heatwave.

Keep in mind that the weather will affect everything in that scene: how people dress, how they walk, how they travel, how they feel.

If you're writing a novel, create some form of a timeline—perhaps month-by-month—showing which scene happens during which part of the year. This will give you a clear idea whether the duel will take place on a crisp cool March morning, under a drizzling February sky, in stormy October or in thick November fog.

If you're revising an already written novel, I recommend developing this kind of timeline as well. Be very aware which season your protagonists are experiencing, and let the reader feel the experience.

For outdoor scenes, the weather needs to affect the action. For indoors scenes, it may only need a passing reference—the rain hammering the windows, the heroine taking off her sodden cloak, the hero turning the lights on.

In historical novels—especially those set in periods before high-speed trains and motorways, before electric lighting and central heating—the weather and the seasons play a crucial role.

PROFESSIONAL EXAMPLES

Overhead, the black clouds boiled and seethed, lightning was striking all around them—waves towered high threatening to break over the bow. (Mercedes Lackey: *Fortune's Fool*)

It was late summer. Rome frizzled like a pancake on a griddleplate. (Lindsey Davis: *The Silver Pigs*)

Even in the shade of the graffiti-carved olive tree, the air sang with heat. (Rayne Hall: *Storm Dancer*)

The sun stabbed at him with lances of fire, and then rising higher bathed the great alkali basin in white radiance and blasting furnace heat. (Louis L'Amour: *Mistakes Can Kill you*)

Beyond the glass, everything was grey and blustered by wind, gulls and white garbage, uninviting.
Staircases of Victorian villas rose to cliffs, and sky full of rain. (Tanith Lee: *When the Lights Go Out*)

The sun started to descend, surfing bright orange waves of heat. Shadows grew longer, while it remained stifling hot. (Lisa Gardner: *The Killing Hour*)

October, fleeting and sappy-sweet with its reddish-gold light and early white frosts and the leaves turning brilliantly, is a different matter, a magical time, a last gleeful defiance in the face of the approaching cold. (Joanne Harris: *Five Quarters of the Orange*)

MISTAKES TO AVOID

Watch out for continuity errors. If your MC walks through the rain in Chapter 4, she needs to be wet when she arrives at her destination in Chapter 5. After several weeks of heavy snow, your MC won't go out without putting on boots, coat and hat. After a hailstorm, the bedraggled petunias will no longer brighten the garden with their colourful glory.

When writing about regions you don't know from personal experience, don't commit stupid blunders by showing weather conditions which don't occur there. A hurricane in central Kansas, a tornado in the Swiss Alps or a monsoon season in Egypt will lessen your credibility with the readers fast (unless the story is about freak weather conditions or climate change).

Don't choose weather to reflect the PoV's mood: The sun smiling when she's in love, a storm roaring when she churns with anger, and rain falling while tears drop from her face, can make your story cheesy. In literary criticism, this obvious use of weather reflecting the mood is called 'The Pathetic Fallacy'. Avoid it.

Instead, choose weather that doesn't obviously reflect the mood, perhaps even weather that's seemingly in contrast, and filter it through the PoV's mood. How does it feel to be newly in love during a hailstorm? How does passionate fury feel when the sea is becalmed and the sun is shining? This makes your writing fresh and original.

ASSIGNMENTS

1. At what time of the year, and what time of the day does this scene take place? What is the weather like at that time in that part of the world?

2. Write several sentences describing the weather. Insert at least two of them in the scene—more may be better. Sprinkle them throughout the scene.

3. Does your work in progress (WiP) have a scene that's lifeless and dull? Consider if a drastic change of weather could bring it to life.

4. What's the weather like where you are right now? Look out of the window or go for a walk. Experience the weather. Observe sounds, sights and smells. Write them down for your Setting Descriptions Bank. You can never have too many weather descriptions.

CHAPTER 6: DETAIL FOR REALISM

A few carefully-chosen visual details create realism and reveal far more about a place than lengthy descriptions.

Mention small things which most people would overlook but which are in some way representative of the place, or of the person who lives there.

A novice might describe a kitchen like this: *It was a medium-sized modern kitchen, approximately five feet wide and twelve feet long, with an oven next to the sink, and a fridge beside the window which had green curtains, and a spice-rack above the fridge. There were three tea-towels hanging from white hooks beside the sink, and there was a lamp hanging from the middle of the ceiling, and on the wall opposite was a calendar.*

A professional writer will use fewer words to say more. Here are five different kitchens, brought to life with two details each:

1. ...the sink overflowing with coffee-cups... a dead wasp on the windowsill

2. ... sparkling chrome water taps... spice jars arranged alphabetically

3. ... famous brand toaster... colour-coordinated tea-towels

4. ... three unopened packs of filter cigarettes ... a pin-up calendar showing a busty blonde and last year's date

5. ... Cookery books titled 'Slim Cuisine', 'Eat Right, Lose Weight Fast' and 'Delicious Low Fat Meals'... a huge chocolate gateau, half eaten

How many visual details should you include? This depends on your individual author voice. For a lean, brisk style, one or two are enough, while a rich, sumptuous style may pamper readers with a dozen.

You may choose to inject more details in places where you want to slow the pace.

HOW AND WHERE TO USE THIS TECHNIQUE

The trick lies in choosing the right details. Here are six areas you may want to explore.

1. What's the ground like? Shining parquet? A carpet with psychedelic pattern and burn holes? Polished marble? Creaking planks? Waterlogged lawn? Patched asphalt? Weed-infested gravel?

2. What are the walls like? Any pictures or graffiti? If yes, what kind? Cracks? Stains? Peeling wallpaper? Patches of mould? Cobwebs in the corners?

3. Are there any posters, notices, signs? These reveal much about the intent of the people who put them up. They can intimidate, annoy, hint at danger or create a sense of irony if other people are obviously ignoring them.

4. Any plants? What kind? In what condition? Neglected or cared-for?

5. Any animals? Pets, cattle, wild birds? How does the animal sit, stand, move? What sounds does it make? A robin may perch on a fencepost and chirp, a seagull may soar overhead and screech, a spider may dangle from the ceiling, a cockroach may scuttle into a floor crack.

6. The source and quality of the light always provides atmospheric details (see Chapter 3).

Insert the details when it is natural for the PoV to notice them.

PROFESSIONAL EXAMPLES

The Dragon and Stars Academy of Martial Arts was located on the second floor of a tired brick building on Harrison Avenue, and as Jane and Frost climbed the narrow stairway, they could hear chants and grunts and thumping feet, and could already smell the sweaty locker-room door. Inside the studio, a dozen students garbed in black pajama-like costumes moved with such total focus that not a single one seemed to notice the two detectives' entrance. Except for a faded martial arts poster, it was a starkly empty room with bare walls and a scuffed wood floor. (Tess Gerritsen: *The Silent Girl*)

Here they sit in the dark oppressive parlour of the vicarage, with its skimpy carpet, faded wallpaper, and stern pictures of former incumbents. (Carol Hedges: *Honour & Obey*)

Afternoon light filtered through filigree lattices, dipping Teruma's study into pale gold. Merida inhaled the cool mint scent.
Barely looking up from the piles of parchment on her desk, Teruma pointed at a yellow divan by the window. Merida plunged onto it, expecting to sink into its sumptuous depth, but beneath its silken softness, it was hard and ungiving. A sleek cat uncurled from an embroidered cushion and stretched, baring claws. Then it yawned and settled back to sleep. A caged bird twittered and fell silent. (Rayne Hall: *Storm Dancer)*

MISTAKES TO AVOID

Don't show details in moments when the PoV wouldn't notice them. For example, a woman running for her life won't look at shop window displays.

Don't give 'maps' and 'floor plans'—the reader probably doesn't need to know that the tower stands sixty feet to the northwest of the gatehouse and that the calendar hangs diagonally across the room from the grandfather clock.

Don't go overboard with details. If you use too many, the reader starts to skip. Choose the most evocative ones. If you want to use more, insert them in different parts of the scene, instead of in one big chunk.

ASSIGNMENTS

1. Think of five details the PoV of your current scene might notice. Choose the two or three most revealing ones, and insert them.

2. Go to a place—perhaps somewhere you need to go anyway, such as the supermarket and the laundrette—and keep your eyes open for telling details. Write them down and file them in your Setting Descriptions Bank.

CHAPTER 7: SIMILES FOR WORLD BUILDING

Describe something by comparing it with something else, and you have a simile. This is a powerful method, because it accomplishes more than just a description. If done well, it reveals something about the PoV's world. Good similes are original, creative, clever and sometimes funny.

HOW AND WHERE TO USE THIS TECHNIQUE

The easiest way to form a simile is with the word 'like'.
... looks like...
.... sounds like....
... smells like ....
...tastes like ...
.... moves like ....
... feels like...
... shaped like...

For example:
The thunder sounded like a giant ripping sheet.
The sky looked grey like bed sheets that had been boil-washed with dirty socks.

Another possibility is using 'as...as':
...as tall as...
...as fast as...
... as small as...
... as pretty as...
... as dark as ...
... as loud as...

You can also use 'than':
... taller than...
... more commanding than...
... smaller than...
... darker than ...
... louder than...

Sometimes 'as if' works well for imaginative similes:

The storm sounded as if someone was slapping wet sheets against the wall.

There are many other ways of constructing a simile. Consider:
... the shape/size/colour of...
...reminded her of...
...reminiscent of...
... enough to...

Compare something in your fiction world with something else from your fiction world, not with something from your own world. If you want to show your reader what the mountains on Planet Alpha Psi look like, don't say they're similar to the Alps, or to the Rocky Mountains (unless your PoV is familiar with the Alps or the Rocky Mountains).

Choose something from within the novel's world. This strengthens the world-building, giving the reader additional rich information about that world, its period and its attitudes.

Examples:

The structure rose as high as the Eiffel Tower.
The structure rose as high as the new tower in Babel.
The structure rose to several times the height of a ship's mast.
The structure rose as high as the new control tower on the Alpha Psi port.

The place was as crowded as a mosque on Saturday.
The place was as crowded as the amphitheatre when Christians fought to the death.
The place was as crowded as McDonald's on a Saturday afternoon.
The place was as crowded as Oxford Street during the January sales.

If possible, choose something that's specific to your PoV's experience. When your PoV encounters something unfamiliar, compare it with something that's familiar to him. This tells the reader a lot about the character's thought processes and background.

This can work well to reveal backstory. These examples reveal something about social background and family:
....*as big as her parents' tennis court....*
... *smelled like the dormitory at the orphanage...*

Similes drawn from the PoV character's job work well. For example, if she's a musician, you can
use many similes about things sounding like music, or being shaped like musical instruments:
...*shaped like a giant harp...*
... *squealed like a tortured violin...*
If your PoV is a historian, use similes related to history:
... *as solid as a Norman stone castle*
... *as ordered as a Roman legion camp...*
If your PoV is a stay-at-home parent, use similes based on parenting:
The items lay strewn on the carpet, as if a pre-schooler had been playing with them.

You can use similes anywhere in your story, but it's best to space them out. Use no more than one or two in a paragraph, unless they're thematically related.

In some fiction genres (such as thrillers), creative similes have become a popular tradition, and readers expect them as part of the reading pleasure.

PROFESSIONAL EXAMPLES

The plants filled the place, a forest of them, with nasty leaves like the newly washed fingers of a dead man. (Raymond Chandler: *The Big Sleep*)

After the darkness of the storm, the building was unnaturally bright, like a television set with the colour turned up too much. (Anthony Horowitz: *Granny*)

Time seeped away like oil from a leaking jar. (Rayne Hall: *Storm Dancer*)

Bare twigs scrape against each other like dry, bony fingers. (Jeni Mills: *The Buried Circle*)

Behind high walls and the evergreen foliage of their gardens, the ugly white façades of several sizeable villas shone through the dark like the faces of the dead. (Jonathan Stroud: *The Amulet of Samarkand*)

Aberdeen Royal Infirmary was spreading like a concrete tumour. For years it'd been in remission, but lately it had started to grow again, infecting the surrounding area with new wings of concrete and steel. (Stuart McBride: *Cold Granite*)

Following the stifled cries and the soft thump, silence sifted down like snowfall. (Dean Koontz, *Intensity*)

The front gardens looked like well-tended family graves planted up with evergreen shrubs, rhododendrons and annuals. (Monika Feth: *The Strawberry Picker*)

... the light of the westering sun was flooding into the cell, splashing like quivering golden water on walls and ceiling. (Rosemary Sutcliff: *The Eagle of the Ninth*)

Across the sea, black shadows race like chariots. (Gene Wolfe: *Soldier of the Mist*)

... upstairs, the carpets are as bald as the head of an Ottoman eunuch. (William Dalrymple: *From the Holy Mountain*)

The room sets me on edge, like a dentist's waiting room, or the room where you wait before a job interview—for a job you don't want. (Kathy Lette: *How to Kill Your Husband and Other Handy Household Hints*)

MISTAKES TO AVOID

Avoid similes in common use *(as dull as ditchwater, as dead as a doornail)* because these clichés make your writing hackneyed and shallow.

Don't cluster several similes into a paragraph unless they're drawn from the same theme. A simile about cookery followed by one about warfare and another about competitive sports is disorienting for the reader. However, a paragraph with several similes about cookery, or about warfare, or about competitive sports can have real power.

Don't use similes outside the PoV's experience. If the PoV is a child living on the edge of the Sahara desert, he won't think that anything looks *like a blanket of snow*, and the Roman legionary won't be reminded of *the sound of a machine gun.*

ASSIGNMENTS

1. For the next few days, try to think in similes. Whenever you visit a place where you don't normally go, look around you and describe the things you see with similes. If you feel creative, you can also describe sounds and smells with similes, although this is more difficult. Compile at least five and add them to your Setting Descriptions Bank.

2. Choose a scene you want to write or revise, preferably one where your PoV is new to a place where she has not been before. See the setting through her eyes. What do the shapes, colours and movements remind her of? Write one or two sentences to insert into your scene.

CHAPTER 8: SYMBOLS FOR THE LITERARY TOUCH

Here's a trick for giving your novel a subtle literary touch—symbolism. When something in the setting reflects something of the story's deeper meaning, it becomes a symbol. This is useful if you want your readers to get a lasting impression of your book, not just momentary entertainment.

HOW AND WHERE TO USE THIS TECHNIQUE

Symbolism is an advanced technique. Skilled writers can use it deftly, but if you're new to fiction writing, it's best to apply it with a light brush.

You may want to try these two approaches and see which of them suits you best:

1. Consider your novel's theme and create symbols to reflect it.

What items in the setting might be symbols for the theme? Describe these items in more detail than other parts of the setting, and show them repeatedly in different ways. Let's say your novel's theme is 'ambition'. What might symbolise this—perhaps a tall office block? You could show such a building repeatedly in your novel. Perhaps in one scene it towers over the townscape, in another its glass front gleams like diamonds, while in a third it gets battered by storms. If it suits the plot, you could even show the building getting built or demolished.

2. Consider the types of setting in your novel, and use them as symbols.

Is there any kind of setting which occurs more than once in your novel? Perhaps several scenes are set in kitchens: Grandma's cosy kitchen, a fast food restaurant kitchen, and the kitchen of an army camp. Or perhaps there are several bridges: Golden Gate Bridge, a railway bridge, and a Japanese-style bridge across a koi pond in the garden. Or several baths: the tin tub with lion's feet from your protagonist' s childhood, and a hammam steam bath during a holiday in Turkey, and the barrel of dirty water serving the washing needs of forty desperate refugees. Whatever recurring setting element you've picked, take a few minutes to brainstorm what it might mean, what kind of symbolism it might have. Freewrite ideas on paper, look up a chart of magical correspondences, search it on the internet, or ask your writing buddies for ideas.

Here are some examples what settings could stand for:
Kitchen = home, warmth, nourishment, family, mother, childhood, centre, safety
Bath = cleanliness, cleansing, ethnic cleansing, washing away guilt, innocence, denial, shedding the past, renewing oneself, relaxing, purification
Bridge = communication, overcoming obstacles, linking separate elements, making connections, bridging gaps between ideologies, healing breaches

From your list of ideas, pick the one which resonates with your story, something which has meaning in the context. Find a way to connect the symbolism with the plot. This will probably be easier than it sounds. The symbolism may already be there, so you merely need to add a few details or to tweak a sentence to emphasise it.

It's not necessary to spell out the symbolism, or for the characters to be aware of it. It's probably best if it's not spelled out. Keep it subtle.

You can have more than one symbol in a novel.

If you write literary fiction, you may want to use this technique a lot. Do it skilfully, and it will make literary reviewers drool. It's the kind of thing which leads to essay assignments: 'Discuss the theme of bridges in the novel ZZZZ by XX YY' and 'Compare and contrast the symbolism of kitchens and baths in ZZZZ'.

In other genres, it's best to apply this technique so lightly that the reader is not consciously aware.

MISTAKES TO AVOID

Don't force symbolism on your story if it doesn't feel right.

ASSIGNMENTS

1. Identify one type of setting that recurs. Create a list of possible symbolic meanings.

2. Expand your descriptions for those settings to make them more interesting and significant.

3. What is your novel's theme? How can you use setting to symbolise an aspect of it?

CHAPTER 9: THE QUANTITY PROBLEM

Setting descriptions make a scene vivid in the reader's mind—but they can also bore the reader more than any other part of the narrative. Many readers skip those paragraphs.

What can you do about this? The solution: make your setting descriptions short and compelling.

Quality and quantity both matter. You need to describe the setting in a way which keeps the reader hooked, and to keep the descriptions so short that the reader won't skip them.

WHICH WEAKNESS IS YOURS?

The 'quantity problem' comes in three variations.

Too Little?

Many writers use nearly no setting descriptions. As a result, their scenes seem to take place in 'white space'. The reader can't see anything and doesn't feel like she's there.

Too Much?

Other writers put great effort into writing lengthy setting descriptions—which the readers skip in order to get on with the story.

A Dump in the Front?

A common weakness of new writers is to describe the setting in detail at the beginning of the scene, and not to mention the setting again for the rest. This leads to readers skipping the early paragraphs and then not feeling connected with the place.

PUT YOUR WRITING TO THE TEST

Take a scene you've written, preferably an advanced 'nearly-there' draft. If possible, choose a scene where the novel visits a place not previously described.

Find all setting descriptions. Highlight them—either with a marker pen on paper or with the highlight function on your computer.

Also highlight all passing references to setting, which are not descriptions but give a clue about the location. For example, in *the wind tousled her hair*, 'the wind' is a clue that it's an outdoor location; highlight 'the wind'. In *she sank back into her chair*, 'her chair' gives a clue about the setting; highlight 'her chair'.

Look at the overall pattern. How are the highlights distributed over the pages? Or do highlights come in big chunks? Maybe there's just one big highlighted block at the beginning? Do the highlights dominate the middle? Do you have no highlights at all?

This pattern gives you, at a glance, an unbiased visual assessment. It tells you how to revise your setting.

The perfect scene has this pattern:

- highlights sprinkled all over the pages
- something highlighted within the first five sentences
- more highlights on the first page than elsewhere
- no long (100+ words) highlighted sections after the first quarter
- no very long (500+ words) blocks of unrelieved highlights anywhere

If the pattern of highlights in your scene differs from the ideal pattern, consider revising it.

SOLUTIONS

How much is too much, depends on your genre and your chosen author voice. Some authors have a terse writing style, and a brief descriptive sentence here and there suits best. Others have a lush, descriptive style where readers bask in the atmosphere of the fictional places. For those, whole paragraphs may be devoted to description.

Either way, avoid long unrelieved stretches of description. Break up the descriptions and insert small pieces throughout the scene.

If You Have Too Little

If your setting descriptions are too sparse, flesh them out by inserting sentences about background noises (see Chapter 2) and the weather (see Chapter 5).

If You Have Too Much

If your setting descriptions are too long, shorten them. Keep only a few particularly evocative sentences and drop the rest. Often it's possible to simply tighten the description, deleting unnecessary detail (we usually don't need detailed floor plans) and removing excess wordage so that every word contributes to a picture.

If you have large chunks of descriptions and then long sections without, split the descriptions into several smaller parts and distribute them throughout the scene.

Integrate the setting descriptions into the action by letting the characters interact with the environment.

No Rules

Your scene doesn't need to follow the 'ideal pattern' precisely. Every story is different, and every author has their own voice. Treat the 'ideal pattern' as a guideline, not a rule.

The trick is to make the setting descriptions brief, but powerful. Strong setting descriptions need only a few words to convey strong images. A powerful 30-word description of the setting is going to be more interesting and has more impact than a 300-word description.

ASSIGNMENT

1. Analyse a scene as above. You may want to repeat the experiment with other scenes you've written.

2. Take a novel in your genre, by a writer you admire. Analyse the book's first scene in the same way. Does the pattern correspond to what I've described as 'ideal'? If not, how does it differ? How well do you think the author's distribution of highlights works?

3. If you belong to a critique group, apply the test to a scene from a manuscript submitted by an inexperienced writer. You may find it easier to assess someone else's writing than your own. Which of the three weaknesses applies?

4. Now compare the three results—the professional author, the inexperienced writer, and you.

When you compare the pattern of highlights of the admired author, and that of the novice, which of the two is closer to what I described as 'ideal'? Does the pattern you highlighted in your own scene resemble the professional pattern, or the novice pattern?

CHAPTER 10: DEEP POV

Through whose eyes, ears and thoughts do you want the reader to experience the scene? Show the setting from this character's perspective.

If ten people walk down the same road, all ten will notice something different. Show the setting in the way this particular character would see it.

HOW AND WHERE TO USE THIS TECHNIQUE

When you visualise the place, pick not the details you would see, but the ones the character would. This way, setting descriptions become part of the characterisation.

Consider these factors:

Job

A character who spends day after day, year after year looking at everything in a certain way will automatically assess everything in this manner, even in his leisure time.

Strolling down a road, the architect sees a row of Victorian terraced houses with bay windows, some with modern double glazing, some with rotting window frames. The health and safety inspector walking down the same road notices the overflowing rubbish bins and the dog turds steaming on the pavement.

Hobbies

What stirs a character's interest? Most people immediately notice anything related to their hobbies.

The animal lover sees people walking their bull terriers and a grey squirrel sitting on a fence.

The hobby gardener sees neglected front gardens, overgrown with borage and brambles, and front steps where potted geraniums have died from neglect. The car enthusiast sees battered Citroens parked on the roadside. The burglar observes that half the houses have intruder alarms and motion-sensor floodlights.

Relationships

A mother sees the unsupervised children playing on the pavement, and broken toys. A young man who has started to date a blonde who drives a red Vauxhall, will see red Vauxhall cars and blondes everywhere.

Obsessions

What does your PoV character obsess about? You can convey his state of mind through setting descriptions.

A local politician desperate to get re-elected observes how many voters probably live in this road, and that potholes and defective street lighting are likely concerns. A recovering drug addict struggling against his cravings notices a smell of marijuana. A woman who is desperate to get pregnant sees mothers pushing prams.

Dominant Sense

Is one sense especially acute in this character, either by nature or by training?

Walking down a rainy road, a vision-oriented painter will see the spreading circles on the surfaces of puddles, while a drummer will hear the rhythm of the drops hammering on the car roofs.

Deepening the PoV

Leave out filter words which create a barrier between the PoV and the reader:

I/he/she/   saw/heard/smelled/noticed/could   see/could hear/could smell etc. Although these words are not wrong, they're not needed once you've established who the PoV character of the scene is. It's best to use them sparingly.

Here are some examples.

Shallow PoV: *She heard a motor whine in the distance.*
Deep PoV: *A motor whined in the distance.*

Shallow PoV: *He realised that the hum came from a combine harvester.*
Deep PoV: *The hum came from a combine harvester.*

Shallow PoV: *He could see waves crashing against the shore.*
Deep PoV: *Waves crashed against the shore.*

The deeper the PoV, the more powerful the reader's experience.

MULTIPLE PoVS

If your story has several PoV characters—perhaps changing with each chapter—change your setting description style with the PoV. For example, your heroine could have a strong sense of smell and notice flowers, textiles and colours while your hero may have acute hearing and observe cars, historical buildings and shapes.

MISTAKES TO AVOID

Don't describe a place the way you would see it.

If your story alternates between several PoV characters, don't let them see their surroundings in the same way.

ASSIGNMENTS

1. Who is the PoV of the scene you're writing or revising? What might he notice most, given his job, hobbies, obsessions and dominant sense? Write a sentence about this.

2. Check your scene draft to see if you can delete any unnecessary *saw*, *heard*, *smelled*, *sensed/could hear*, *could see*, *could smell*, *could sense* and similar phrases.

CHAPTER 11: OPENING SCENES

Two hundred years ago, leisurely openings with detailed setting descriptions were popular. Authors could describe a landscape over several pages before introducing the character or starting the plot. Modern readers have less patience. They want to get to the exciting part fast.

You can still start your story with a description of the setting—indeed, this can be one of the most effective openings—but you need to make the setting description part of the story. The reader must feel that events are already underway.

Alternatively, begin with something else—dialogue or action perhaps - and insert small clues about the setting.

HOW TO USE THIS TECHNIQUE

Show the setting through the eyes of the PoV character. Make it clear as soon as possible (probably in the first two paragraphs) who the PoV is, why he's in this place, what he wants, and how the setting affects him and his goal.

Let the character interact with the setting. He may walk, work or search something there.

Similes are a useful technique for opening scenes. By comparing something in the setting with something from the PoV's background you can tell the reader something about this character in a quick and subtle way. (See Chapter 7.)

Introduce the conflict and start the action soon (on the first page, if the story allows it) and try to weave the description and the action together.

If you start with the setting, choose a location which is unusual, to make the reader curious. It should also be characteristic of your novel, because the beginning makes a promise to the reader: "This is the kind of experience you'll get if you read this book."

Interesting weather—heavy fog, icy wind, pouring rain, blistering heat—can help the reader identify with the PoV character's experience from the start.

When you start your story with something other than the setting, insert some clues about the location early on, to avoid the feeling of 'white space'. Background noises (see Chapter2), light effects (Chapter 3), smells (Chapter 1) and the weather (Chapter 5) provide useful clues without taking up much space.

PROFESSIONAL EXAMPLES

Here are examples of novels starting with the setting.

Cassius Quintius Corbulo nudged his horse towards the side of the alley, taking them both out of the glare of the bright morning sun. (Nick Brown: *The Siege*)

Snowflakes dazzle against the evening sky and fall gentle around this stark tower. (Susan Fraser King: *Lady Macbeth*)

Near winter's end, the man walked by the sea's edge. The sky was pale and low and calm, the water almost still, like silvered mirror, and meeting the pebbled beach, slow like cream. (Tanith Lee: *When the Lights Go Out*)

MISTAKES TO AVOID

Don't start the story with a long chunk of setting description without character, conflict or action. Such an opening lacks a hook, and few agents, editors or readers will bother to read on.

Avoid the beginning where a character drives/walks/rides through a landscape, and along the way observes the fauna, flora and architecture of the place, reflects on its social and political history, contemplates his purpose and reflects on his life so far. Novice writers often start this way, but it doesn't hook readers.

ASSIGNMENT

1. What happens in the first scene? What would be the best place where you could set the scene—a location that's both unusual and typical for the novel?

2. Write some sentences of setting description for this scene, including sounds and smells. Write them from the PoV character's perspective.

3. Write or revise the first 500 words of your novel or story. Either focus on the setting, and insert clues about the PoV character, his goal and the conflict. Or focus on action, dialogue or something else, and insert clues about the setting.

You may want to write several different openings, then choose the one with the strongest potential to hook the reader.

CHAPTER 12: CLIMAX SCENES

The climax scene is the most exciting part of your novel. Enhance the excitement by setting this scene in a dramatic place.

HOW TO USE THIS TECHNIQUE

Choose an unusual location—perhaps even one which is dangerous. How about a derelict rollercoaster, a rainforest canopy, a sheer rock face, or an abandoned mineshaft?

In a novel, the climax may happen in a place the MC has previously avoided because it's so dangerous. Now he has no choice, because the villain has imprisoned him there or because it's where he must go to save the world.

You can also choose a location which is normally pleasant, and where the MC has spent previous happy scenes. But at the novel's climax, something terrible happens: the ship sinks. The skyscraper is on fire. The dam is about to burst. The tide comes rolling in and threatens to sweep everything away.

This will enhance the thrill of the action.

Another way to layer the excitement of the climax scene is to add extreme weather—a hurricane, a blizzard, a hailstorm. For ideas, see Chapter 5.

If you really want to grip your readers with a thrilling climax, think about what your MC fears. Does she have a phobia of heights or of fire? Is she terrified of snakes or of drowning? Whatever scares her, if she has successfully avoided it during the novel, during the climax she must confront this fear. The only way to survive and to rescue her loved ones is to enter the burning building, to scale the cliff, to dive through the submerged corridor or to jump into the snake pit.

MISTAKES TO AVOID

Don't choose a blandly pleasant setting for the climax, such as sunny meadow or a comfortable restaurant.

If your MC has to confront a phobia during the novel's climax, don't mention it for the first time in that scene. Mention it several times before, or better still, show her successfully avoiding the danger.

ASSIGNMENTS

1. Think of the most exciting novels you've read and movies you've watched. Can you remember the climax scenes and their settings? Were the locations dangerous in some way?

2. Take the climax scene you have drafted for your novel and want to revise, or think about the climax scene you want to plot. What would be an exciting location? Could you enhance the drama or danger of the place?

3. Optional for thrillers, horror and other excitement-rich genres: What fear does your MC have? In what kind of place will she be forced to confront this fear?

CHAPTER 13: ACTION SCENES

When the story action is fast—for example, during chases and fights—the writing needs to convey the speed. Setting descriptions are problematic here, because they slow the pace.

When the PoV character is in a hurry, she won't pause to contemplate the scenery, and when she's fighting for her life, she can't afford to divert her attention to her surroundings.

Yet these scenes need setting—otherwise they happen in 'white space' and don't feel real.

HOW TO SHOW THE SETTING WITHOUT SLOWING THE PACE

1. Establish the setting beforehand. If the reader is already familiar with the terrain, you only need to mention items in the setting without describing them.

2. Show only what the PoV character sees in this situation. These are probably things nearby or relevant to her plans.

3. Let the PoV character move through the setting, and describe only what she interacts with:

She groped her way along the icy wall.
Gravel crunched under his boots.
She raced down the darkened alley, past overflowing dustbins and graffiti-sprayed façades.

4. Use the setting to create obstacles for the action. Make your characters leap across walls, duck behind desks, skid on icy roads.

5. Use sounds to increase the excitement. They don't slow the pace the way visuals do.

6. Use short words, and mostly short- to medium-length sentences. Avoid words of more than three syllables and sentences of more than twenty words.

7. Use powerful verbs and nouns to carry the description, and use few—if any—adjectives and adverbs.

CHASES

During chases, the PoV pays little attention to the scenery, whether he is the pursuer or the pursued. At the same time, the setting is crucial for these scenes.

Here are some suggestions:

1. Describe what the ground is like. The running/driving/riding person notices this, because it affects their progress.

2. Show obstacles—anything the character needs to leap across, scramble up, duck under, cling to.

3. Mention the sounds of the chase, for example tyres squealing on the tarmac, hooves clopping on the cobbled street, boots thudding on the concrete.

4. The pursued may scan what's before him to identify an escape route or a hiding place.

5. Show the setting as part of the character's movements and endeavours, not in static descriptions.

6. Don't describe colours and light effects, or use similes in chase scenes.

7. Use short words, especially vivid verbs and nouns. As far as possible, avoid long words, long sentences, and adverbs.

FIGHTS

Many writers find fight scenes challenging to write. Choosing an interesting location—a place where the reader wouldn't expect a fight to happen—helps make the fight scene memorable.

How does the space affect the fighting? Perhaps the ceiling means the fighter can't swing his sword as high as he's accustomed to, or the spiralling staircase gives the right-handed attacker almost no room to swing his sword. Maybe a fighter leaps onto the bar, or smashes his opponent into a wall. Find a way to incorporate the setting into the fight.

Few terrains are even. If there's a slope, then the fighter who stands higher up has the advantage over his opponent below.

What's the ground like? This will affect the fighting. Will the fighters' feet sink into the soggy morass? Will they slip on iced-over asphalt? Does the clay soil of the freshly-ploughed field cling to their boots and slow their moves? When your PoV falls, does he land on hard concrete, on a silken rug, or in inch-deep manure?

Describe the setting before the action starts. Once the fighting is underway, your MC can't afford to take his attention off the fight for even a moment, so any setting description during the fight would feel unnatural.

MISTAKES TO AVOID

Don't pause the action to insert setting descriptions.

During a battle, don't let your PoV character know how his comrades on the side of the battlefield are faring. He is too occupied to look.

ASSIGNMENTS

1. Select a scene in your WiP where the action is fast. Think of several parts of the setting which can become part of the action.

2. Write sentences in which your MC interacts with the setting during this scene—for example, he leaps across a fence or scales a cliff face.

CHAPTER 14: SPOOKY, SCARY, SUSPENSEFUL SCENES

Setting descriptions are perfect for creating a spooky atmosphere and making your reader bite her nails with suspense..

Here are some techniques you can use:

1. To make a scene spooky or scary, dip the place in near-darkness. It's a deep-seated human instinct to be nervous in the dark, and as writers, we can play with that. Perhaps you can choose a dark location, such as a forest at night or an unlit cave. You could also let the campfire burn down, the torch battery go flat, a power cut turn off all lights, or the wind blow out the candle. Darkness reduces the vision, so use the other senses more, especially the sense of hearing.

For ideas how to describe a night-time setting, see Chapter 16.

2. To create a sense of unease and foreboding, mention and describe shadows. Show how the shadows creep along the walls, how they swallow the bright details, how they reach like tentacles into the room. Shadows are also great if you want to evoke an eerie, spooky mood.

3. Moving, flickering, disappearing and reappearing lights also add to a spooky effect. Describe the way the candle flickers or the way clouds ghost across the moon.

4. Sounds create excitement, and can intensify a feeling of danger and fear. If you want to make a scene be spooky, suspenseful or scary, insert many descriptions of sounds throughout that scene. For ideas, see Chapter 2.

5. Similes are a great way to build foreboding, long before the bad thing happens. Use similes to compare something innocuous in the landscape with something ominous. See Chapter 7 for suggestions.

6. The colours red and black strike a chord deep in the reader's subconscious, evoking primal instincts of danger. Consider showing red and black items in the surroundings, and if possible describe these colours creatively. See Chapter 4.

7. To ratchet up the suspense, let the character enter through a door on the way to danger. To the reader's subconscious, this represents a final barrier, the last chance to stay safe. Describe the door in one or several sentences—for example its appearance, how the doorknob feels in the character's palm, and what it sounds like when it opens.

8. If you plan to record your story as a podcast or audiobook, or if you plan to give public readings, use euphonic effects: 's' and 'ee' sounds create spookiness, while 'ow' evokes foreboding and 'oo' doom.

10. Changes in temperature can intensify tension, suspense and fear. A gradual drop in temperature is most effective, but intense heat can also bring matters to a boiling point.

11. At the beginning of the scary scene, add hints of danger... a barbed wire fence, a sign 'Warning. Keep Out'.

12. Use the setting to isolate the characters from any help: no mobile phone reception in the valley, steep cliffs which can't be scaled, a river infested with crocodiles, a flood that has washed away the boats, snowdrifts blocking the road.

13. Use the weather (see Chapter 5) to increase the isolation further. The character can't leave the cave or the hut because there's a snowstorm raging outside. She can't cross the river because the bridge has collapsed, and she can't light a signal fire because the wood won't burn in the torrential rain.

MISTAKES TO AVOID

Don't tell the reader that the place is spooky/eerie/scary. Show it.

ASSIGNMENTS

1. Which of the thirteen suggestions could work for your scene? Select several.

2. Write one to three sentences describing a door your character walks through on her way to danger. This can be a conventional door, a garden gate, a castle gatehouse, a trapdoor or whatever suits your scene.

3. What noises can be heard in this location? Write a sentence describing one or several sounds.

CHAPTER 15: LOVE SCENES

In love scenes, the writer seeks to stir the reader's emotions. Make them feel the PoV character's need, longing, tenderness, affection, desire, passion, pain, hope or despair.

The setting can help rouse emotions and make the love scene memorable.

Consider a location that's unusual, dramatic, wild. What's the wildest part of nature in that area? How about setting the scene on a windswept moorland, or on a wave-lashed cliff?

If you place the love scene in a remote place, the fact that the two are the only people around can create a bond between them that hadn't previously existed, and it can also encourage confidences.

The outdoors can add to the romance of the situation. The vastness of open space may emphasise the closeness of the couple.

Settings can force two people closer together than they would otherwise choose to be, and a skilled writer can use this for the plot. Perhaps two people who dislike each other are trapped in a small air pocket in an earthquake-collapsed building and must cooperate to ensure their survival, or two strangers shelter from a hurricane in a cave that's so small they can't avoid touching.

For an important love scene, especially if it's in the final third of the novel, a danger-filled setting works well. Perhaps the pair are standing on the deck of a sinking ship, or sheltering in a feeble hut that may get swept away any moment by the violent gale.

The weather serves well to magnify emotions. Even something simple, such as a sudden downpour drenching the characters, adds interest. For ideas, see Chapter 5.

Think cinematic ally. What kind of setting would look awesome in a movie? Perhaps the lovers watch as flames engulf their ancestral home, or they stand on the roof of a tall building gazing down on the night-lit city, or are climbing a craggy rock face surrounded by majestic mountains.

Love scenes can also have a 'tame' setting, such as a cosy cabin with a deep-pile wool rug in front of a crackling log fire, where the aroma of coffee mingles with the scent of wood resin. This works especially well if the characters have just survived a dangerous adventure, and you want to give them (and the reader) a short rest before you put them through the next ordeal. Use the setting to create pleasant sensations for several senses—touch, taste, temperature and smell as well as vision and hearing.

If you use the 'Scene & Sequel' approach to structuring, you may want to make the setting for the Scene part wild and for the Sequel cosy.

For erotic scenes, consider unusual settings. In real life, most people would choose comfortable, safe, private spaces to have sex. In fiction, you can spice up your scene by doing the opposite. What's a weird space? Could it be slightly uncomfortable? Is it a semi-public space where they might get spotted at any moment?

In the grip of passion, a couple may have sex before reaching the bedroom. Some couples may deliberately choose an unromantic and uncomfortable venue for their tryst, such as the dungeon beneath a castle ruin, while others may have sex in the boss's office or an aeroplane because they get a thrill from the risk of discovery.

They may be willing to put up with some discomfort, or find a way to be comfortable—but keep it realistic. The action needs to be physically possible in that space. Readers won't believe a threesome in an aircraft toilet that has scarcely room for one passenger.

At the beginning of the erotic scene, use the setting to activate the reader's senses for the hot action that's to come. Focus especially on the sense of touch: what does the ruined castle wall feel like when the heroine leans against it? How does the wind feel on her cheeks? The bed's satin sheets on her breasts?

PROFESSIONAL EXAMPLES

The storm had ebbed a little, but the wind was still blowing a gale as they stepped outside. Lynne pulled the hood of her jacket up over her head, waiting at the bottom of the steps as Rhys locked the door of the boathouse—he had kept his yellow oilskin coat on over his dinner jacket, the collar turned up against the wind.

The waves were still pounding against the rocks below them, churning around the bottom of the lifeboat ramp, where the boat was still tied up and dancing on her ropes as she rode out the worst of the weather. Lynne walked over to the rail, fascinated by the sheer power of the untamed elements. The salt spray was stinging cold against her face, but she didn't care—it made her feel as if she were almost part of it, the wild turmoil of the sea matching the turmoil of emotions in her heart. (Susanne McCarthy: *Her Personal Bodyguard*)

It was a beautiful night. There was no moon; the sea was like black silk, seamed by the white lacy froth of their wake, the sky was inky velvet spangled with a million stars. She had never seen so many stars, the lofty sweep of the milky-way curving down to the far horizon, invisible in the darkness.

She leaned against the rail, gazing out at the sky. The cool night breeze tugged at her hair, the only sound was the soft swish of the waves rushing beneath the white hull. There was no land in sight, no other boats. With only their running-lights showing, they were all alone on the vast empty expanse of water. It was as if they were chasing the stars across the wide Mediterranean Sea...

(Susanne McCarthy: *Chasing Stars*)

MISTAKES TO AVOID

Many novice writers think that romance can happen only in romantic locations, and tenderness is only possible in gentle settings.

In romantic and erotic scenes, avoid unpleasant odours. Those are a turn-off for the reader.

ASSIGNMENT

1. Choose a location for an important love scene you're revising, writing or planning. What wild nature is nearby? In what quirky place could the action develop? Can you surround the lovers with danger and drama? If this doesn't suit your story, think of a cosy setting in which the characters can feel comfortable and safe.

CHAPTER 16: NIGHT SCENES

Events during the night can be especially exciting, romantic or scary—but you need to use a different approach to description.

Use different senses. In the dark or semi-dark, your PoV character won't see much, so use the sense of vision less and the other senses more.

The sense of hearing is especially important. Insert several background noises.

At night, most people's sense of smell becomes heightened, so you may want to mention the scents and odours of the place. However, this depends on the temperature. If the night is cold, the smells won't be as noticeable as during a balmy evening. (See Chapter 1 for ideas how to use smells.)

If the scene takes place outdoors, show the weather and the temperature, and show in detail how they affect the characters and the action. (See Chapter 5.)

Any lights, whether nearby or faraway, will be noticeable at night, so mention lights. Here are some ideas:

- car headlights
- street lamps (a row of them or a single one)
- lit windows in houses
- the glowing tip of a cigarette
- the stars (unless the sky is cloudy)
- the moon (full, waxing, waning, crescent, gibbous?)
- a campfire
- lanterns
- torches
- the hazy cloud of light above a distant city
- any appliances in use (a tablet, a mobile phone)

Describe the colour, quality and movement of the light. Use your full creativity to come up with original, atmospheric descriptions. (See Chapter 3 for more ideas.)

In an indoors scene, mention drawn curtains. Show the soft glow of the candles, the sparkles of the chandelier, the irritating flicker of the strip light.

Fear, danger, anxiety, uncertainty, are increased in the dark. By emphasising the darkness, you can create suspense and fear. For more about this, see Chapter 14.

PROFESSIONAL EXAMPLES

Here are some brief excerpts from night scenes.

A smear of harsher light in the lower left corner of the window was flung from the faltering streetlamps of South Jackson. The light striated across the cracked window, destroying even his memories of the blessed empty darkness of true night. Sweet night of star-speckled skies and tree-breathed air had been replaced by a crouching greyness that emanated from the city. It came as much from the gutters and dumpsters as from headlights and streetlamps.
(Megan Lindholm: *The Wizard of the Pigeons*)

The house was black on black, only a faint crooked line of stars where the roof ended and the sky began. It seemed bigger and intangible, edges blurring, ready to dissolve into nothing if you came too close. The lit windows looked too warm and gold to be real, tiny pictures beckoning like old peep shows (...) The a cloud skated off the moon.... (Tana French: *The Likeness*)

The squat was halfway down a terrace of abandoned two-storey buildings—dirty granite walls barely lit by the dull streetlights, windows covered with thick plywood. Except for one on the upper floor, where a thin, sick-looking light oozed out through the dirty glass, accompanied by thumping dance music. Rosie Williams died the way she'd lived: ugly. Lying on her back in the cobbled alley, staring up at the orange-grey night sky, the drizzle making her skin sparkle, gently washing the dark red blood from her face. (Stuart McBride: *Dying Light*)

They stepped out into the predawn gloom, lit only by the diffuse glow of city lights. Shining her flashlight, Jane saw a plastic table and chairs, flowerpots of herbs. On a sagging clothesline, a full load of laundry danced like ghosts in the wind. (Tess Gerritsen: *The Silent Girl*)

Outside it is a moonlit night. But the moon, being past the full, is only now rising over the wilderness of London. Everything is still. Still in gardens and parks, still upon smoky hills and highways, still upon steeples and towers, and trees with a grey ghost of bloom upon them. (Carol Hedges: *Honour & Obey*)

MISTAKES TO AVOID

Beginner writers often fail to create a convincing night-time experience because they don't use the senses enough. Remember to use the senses of hearing, touch, smell and temperature, as well as other senses, such as taste, if relevant to the context.

ASSIGNMENTS

1. Go out at night—perhaps to a place that resembles a location in your WiP, or somewhere bizarre. If you dare, visit a cemetery at midnight, or walk through a rough neighbourhood. For your safety, you may want to bring along your dog or an understanding friend. But even your own back garden can yield interesting material. Absorb the lights, smells and noises of the place. Collect as many observations as possible and add them to your Setting Descriptions Bank.

2. Imagine the location of your night scene. What smells might the PoV character notice? How does the ground feel underfoot? What noises can be heard in the background? Write five sentences about the setting that don't involve the sense of seeing, and sprinkle them throughout your scene.

CHAPTER 17: OUTDOOR SCENES

If your scene takes place outdoors, the location can enrich the plot. The characters may appear or feel small in the vast landscape, helpless, overwhelmed and lost. Nature—sometimes unpredictable, sometimes inevitable—shapes events.

Outdoors settings often work well for quests (e.g. the hero must find the hermit who lives in the forest), explorations (e.g. the archaeologists excavating an ancient temple), searches (e.g. the police team with dogs searching for a body in the woods), love scenes (e.g. the doomed lovers meet on the windswept moor), and battles (two medieval armies clash in the blistering desert heat).

For an outdoors scene, make sure you involve the weather, and show how it affects the characters and the actions. Which direction does the wind come from? How strong is it? What's the temperature like? Does the rain hit the PoV from the front or from behind? For more ideas how to use the weather, see Chapter 5.

What does the sky look like? Describe its colour—if possible in more imaginative ways than 'blue' or 'grey' and the pattern of clouds. Be creative, because descriptions of the sky can serve to establish the PoV's mood and may even foreshadow events.

Where does the sun stand in the sky—in what direction, and how high? How bright or sparse is the sunlight? How sharp and how long are the shadows? What hue does the sunlight give to the surroundings—does it gild everything with a warm glow, does it create stark contrasts? The location of the sun and the quality of the sunlight not only conjure atmosphere, but give clues to the season and the time of the day.

What's the ground like? Is the asphalt dotted white with seagull droppings, or black with old chewing gum? Are the paving-slabs cracked, lichen-encrusted or worn smooth? What sounds do the PoV's footsteps make? Is the lawn shorn short, or tangled with weeds? Is the ploughed field so soggy that clumps of clay soil attach themselves to the walker's boots, or is it baked hard in the dry heat?

In urban locations, what kind of rubbish lies on the ground— empty beer cans, used condoms, or apple cores? What kind of graffiti are sprayed on the walls?

How are the lawns and gardens kept? Do tulips stand in orderly rows, or do weeds choke the gardens? What are the weeds—brambles with their thorny tentacles, sycamore seedlings plotting to turn the garden into a dense wood in a few short years, or dandelions cheerfully resisting the gardener's strict regime?

What kind of trees grow in the place? Pines, pears or poplars? Are they winter-bare, verdant with young leaves, laden with fruit, or gilded with autumn? Tall or dwarfing, sparse or lush, stunted from continued severe winds or crippled by an overzealous gardener's pruning shears?

What sounds are created by the environment? Cars humming/roaring/whining past?
Leaves rustling overhead? Twigs breaking as an unseen animal steps on them? The outdoors is never completely silent. If you want to emphasise a sense of silence, do it by describing a faraway noise (for example, the distant howl of a coyote).

What animals can be seen or heard? Dogs splashing in the brook, a cat lazing on the low wall, or an owl hooting in the distance? Do birds twitter, chirp, screech?

Outdoor scenes need smells, unless it is very cold. What does the air smell of? Bonfire smoke? Lilies in bloom? Freshly mowed grass? Petrol fumes?

PROFESSIONAL EXAMPLES

As I walked towards home the streets became clamorous, with traders' cries, hoofbeats and harness bells. A small black dog, his fur clinging in spiked clumps barked madly at me as I passed a baker's shop. (Lindsey Davis: *The Silver Pigs*)

The light from the yet unrisen sun flowed softly gold and rose between the long blue shadows of the village houses and across the fields and hedgerows full of birdsong. (Margaret Frazer: *The Midwife's Tale*)

Merida marched fast, pretending to have a purpose. Darkness fell fast, and nothing remained of the day except lingering heat. The inn near the bridge had a huge canine painted on its façade, next to a sign promising Darrian Dansers Evry Night, *complete with a drawing of a female torso with unrealistic curves. The clacking steps of spear-armed guards drove Merida into the inn's courtyard where camels slurped from a trough. A smell of jasmine was even stronger than the reek of animal sweat and dung. Torches waved their yellow flames in the descending gloom.* (Rayne Hall: *Storm Dancer*)

On the thirteenth of April in the year 1785 I was sitting in a ditch in Derbyshire, convinced I was dying. The ditch was unremarkable: a straggly hawthorn hedge behind, a damp stony bottom full of the usual crawly things, a fringe of grass in front and beyond that the rutted road. (...) On a hawthorn twig above my head the robin, careless of my probable fate, sang his song to the patch of blue sky that showed between the heavy clouds moving away to the east. (Mary Brown: *Playing the Jack*)

When I landed on top of a lamppost in the London dusk it was peeing with rain. This was just my luck. I had taken the form of a blackbird, a sprightly fellow with a bright yellow beak and jet-back plumage. Within seconds I was as bedraggled a fowl as ever hunched its wings in Hampstead. Flicking my head from side to side I spied a large beech tree across the street. Leaves mouldered at its foot—it had already been stripped clean by the November winds—but the thick sprouting of its branches offered some protection from the wet. I flew over to it, passing above a lone car that purred its way along the wide suburban road. Behind high walls and the evergreen foliage of their gardens, the ugly white façades of several sizeable villas shone through the dark like the faces of the dead. (Jonathan Stroud: *The Amulet of Samarkand*)

MISTAKES TO AVOID

Don't write outdoors scenes without specific weather. They lack realism.

Don't forget to show the sun (or the clouds hiding the sun), the wind (even if it's only a faint breeze) and the temperature.

ASSIGNMENTS

1. Go somewhere out of doors—take your dog for a walk in a municipal park, or sunbathe on the beach, or have a cup of tea in a pavement cafe—and observe the light, sounds, smells, wind, weather, ground and sky. Jot down your observations and add them to your Settings Description Bank.

2. For the outdoors scene you want to write or revise, decide the location, season, time of the day and weather. Write one sentence each about the sunlight, ground, sky, weather and temperature, to insert into the scene.

CHAPTER 18: INDOOR SCENES

Indoor scenes are an opportunity for characterisation. By describing the place, you can reveal a lot about the people who built and furnished the place, or who inhabit and use it now, their purposes, habits, tastes and personalities. Think of everything in the room as an extension of the inhabitants' character.

By showing relevant details, you give your PoV character—and your reader—an impression of that person, perhaps even in ways you could not achieve otherwise. For example, a homicide detective can learn about the murder victim's personality and lifestyle by taking in details of his living quarters. A potential investor can draw conclusions about how well the business is run.

As soon as the PoV character enters a new room, show what the place smells of, mentioning one or several characteristic odours. (See Chapter 1.) Then reveal a few visual details, but not many. Aim to capture the feel of the place rather than give a full description. (See Chapter 6).

For interiors of any kind, describe the floor (wooden planks, bare concrete, a threadbare carpet, ethnic rugs?) and the ceiling (any cracks, cobwebs or patches of damp up there?) Is the furniture antique or modern, hand-crafted or flat-pack, functional or ornamental, Spartan or ostentatious? What kind of stuff is lying around—a piece of needlework in an embroidery frame, a baby's feeding bottle, unwashed plates, takeaway cartons, smelly socks? What items are on display—travel souvenirs, status symbols, professional certificates or sporting trophies? What books are on the shelves? Mention a couple of titles—*Das Kapital* or *The Geography of the Bible? Fifty Shades of Grey* or *Huckleberry Finn?* Do the houseplants have glossy green leaves, or are they brown and brittle with neglect, or infested with aphids?

For restaurant scenes, use description to make this an individual place, not a generic eatery. A sentence listing several smells establishes what kind of food they serve. Describe the surface of the tables—starched white linen, shiny metal, cracked plastic or scarred wood? How are the menus presented? Leather-bound books, laminated sheets sticky to the touch, or a chalk board with spelling errors above the counter? What clothes do the servers wear—jeans and t-shirts, black dresses and lace-edged aprons, or miniskirts and cleavage-baring tops? Mention background noises—the hiss of the coffee maker, the rattling of cutlery, the bubbling of hot grease. If there's any music, mention the volume and style. You can also mention snatches of overheard conversations.

When describing a workshop, office or factory, show the tools of the trade, preferably in motion. Mention smells. Almost every workplace has its characteristic smells—of resin, leather, wax, grease, diesel, disinfectant, printer's ink, coffee. If work is underway, describe sounds—machines rattling, hammers clanking, printers whirring, monitors beeping.

PROFESSIONAL EXAMPLES

Here are some excerpts where the PoV character gets an insight into the people who live in these rooms.

Justin, sort of unexpectedly, turned out to have minimalist tastes. There was a small nest of books and photocopies and scribbled pages beside his bedside table, and he had covered the back of his door with photos of the gang—arranged symmetrically, in what looked like chronological order, and covered with some kind of clear sealant—but everything else was spare and clean and functional: white bedclothes, white curtains blowing, dark furniture polished to a shine, neat rows of balled-up socks in the drawers and glossy shoes at the bottom of the wardrobe. The room smelled, very faintly, of something cypressy and masculine. (Tana French: *The Likeness*)

As wealthy as he was, Donahue had depressingly pedestrian taste, something that was apparent as soon as Jane walked into the house and saw the bland pastel paintings hanging on the wall. They looked like mass-produced landscapes for sale at every local shopping mall. Her escorts led her into the living room where an enormous man, bloated as a toad, sat in an extra-large armchair. (Tess Gerritsen: *The Silent Girl*)

Bobby walked deeper into the apartment, doing his best to scope out the place while he had the chance. First impressions: small, cramped main room leading to a small, cramped bedroom. Kitchen was about the size of his bedroom closet, strictly utilitarian, with plain white cupboards and cheap Formica countertops. Family room was slightly larger, boasting a plush green love seat, oversize reading chair, and a small wooden table that also doubled as a work space. Walls were painted a rich golden yellow. Two expanses of enormous eight-foot-high window were trimmed out with scalloped shades made from a sunflower-covered fabric.
As for any other features of the room, they were obscured by piles of fabric. Reds, greens, blues, golds, florals, stripes, checks, pastels. Silk, cotton, linen, chenille. Bobby didn't know a lot about these things, but he was guessing there was about any fabric you could ever want somewhere in this room. (Lisa Gardner: *Hide*)

Her room, like Ryan's, looked as if someone had strategically placed sticks of dynamite in the drawers, blowing them open; some clothes sprawled dead on the flour, others lay wounded midway, clinging to the armoire like the fallen on a barricade before the French Revolution. (Harlan Coben: *Caught*)

MISTAKES TO AVOID

Don't set your scenes in generic places, as if every living room/factory/office was the same.

Avoid giving wordy descriptions showing everything in the room; instead focus on revealing details.

Don't only rely on visual descriptions—mention sounds or smells.

ASSIGNMENTS

1. Focus on the personality of the person who lives or works in the room you're about to describe. What kind of furniture and decorations would he choose, and how would he arrange them? Is he likely to keep his room meticulously tidy, or in slovenly disorder? Write a description of the place with many details. Later, select the most revealing details to use in your story.

2. Visit a place similar to the room where the scene is set, observe and take notes. This exercise will probably yield a wealth of inspiring details you could not have thought of. For a hospital scene, go to a hospital. For a factory scene, go to a factory. If it's not possible or practical to go to the kind of place you need, pick the nearest equivalent. For example, if you want to write about an Anglo-Saxon alehouse, go to your local pub for a drink.

CHAPTER 19: THE PICTURESQUE, THE BEAUTIFUL AND THE SUBLIME

This chapter invites you to look at landscape from a new perspective—or rather, an old one—and pass the impressions on to your readers.

People in the 19th century loved landscapes. Victorians demonstrated their good taste by adorning their homes with landscape paintings. Sketching landscapes was a popular pastime and an important accomplishment for young ladies. Tour guides specialised in showing local beauty spots so the ladies and gents could picnic there, and do some sketching, and maybe compose a poem or two.

These people saw attractive scenery in three categories—picturesque, beautiful, and sublime—and they attached this mental label before they applied a brush to their sketchpad or thought of the first line of a poem.

Thinking like a 19th century person may open up new vistas for your landscape descriptions.

PICTURESQUE

This is a scenery which entices through its harmonious composition. A 19th century person would see this and think 'this landscape would make a great picture' or even 'this landscape is a picture'. The appeal is purely visual—sounds and smells are unimportant—and it doesn't have to be beautiful, just interesting.

A picturesque landscape contains both natural and man-made elements, for example a meadow and a farmhouse, a stream and a ruin, a lake and a sailing boat, a valley and a bridge.

A 19th century gentleman on a walking tour might come across a landscape of rolling hills, framed by tall trees, with a rustic farmhouse in the middle background, and everything arranged in a harmonious composition, and exclaim "How picturesque!" He would, of course, take out his sketchpad to capture the view.

People were so keen on the picturesque that those with power and wealth changed the landscape. If a view was almost perfect, but the stream was too far on the left, they rerouted the stream. One could not let nature spoil the picturesque.

Ruins could be picturesque, if they happened to be in the right spot. Since ruins seldom occurred in the right spot, in the right colour and shape, people built ruins. Everyone worth his wealth and fashion had a 'ruin' on his land, picturesquely positioned of course, with colours and shapes complementing the natural landscape. Fake ruins were big business in the 19th century.

BEAUTIFUL

This is a landscape or landscape feature which gives intense pleasure and satisfies the senses—and not just the visual sense. Perhaps there's a pleasant flower smell, or pleasant birdsong, or the pleasant tinkling of a stream... the emphasis is on 'pleasant'.

A beautiful landscape feature can be natural (a flowery meadow), or man-made (a garden, a temple). It is often fragile, vulnerable, at risk, something which might get destroyed.

SUBLIME

A sublime landscape is all natural without man-made features, big, wild, untamed, dangerous. Think of craggy mountains, gleaming glaciers, sheer rock faces, icebergs, waves crashing against cliffs, rivers racing through canyons, huge waterfalls, windswept moors.

The weather often enhances the sublime experience.

The sublime is not just visual but can be an experience for several senses, so include sounds and smells, as well as temperature   and   touch.

The emotion created by the sublime is awe. It may also evoke fear, excitement or passion. The viewer may or may not experience pleasure.

MISTAKES TO AVOID

If you write historical fiction set in the 19th century, don't ignore these labels. Your PoV character won't be authentic unless he views the landscapes in those terms.

Don't make all the landscapes in your novel picturesque, or beautiful, or sublime. Alternate between the three types, otherwise it can become boring.

When describing beautiful scenery, don't use the word 'beautiful' because to the modern reader, the word doesn't have the same meaning and may seem dull.

ASSIGNMENTS

1. Is the landscape where you live (or near where you live) picturesque, beautiful or sublime? Where is the nearest sublime feature?

2. Train your mind. Next time you go for a walk or a drive, watch out for any beautiful, picturesque or sublime spots.

3. Does your WiP feature any landscapes? If yes, which landscapes could you describe as picturesque, beautiful, or sublime?

CHAPTER 20: THE PASSING OF TIME

Setting descriptions are a great way to cue the reader about how much time has passed.

You don't even need to write 'After four hours', 'It was nine in the evening', 'Six months later'—such statements are fine in official reports, but boring in fiction. Simply show what has changed.

This technique works especially well to orient the reader at the beginning of a new scene as to how much time has passed since the previous one.

Here are some suggestions.

HOURS HAVE PASSED

Show the sun in a different position in the sky. East or west? High up or near the horizon?
The shadows have shortened or lengthened.
The sunlight has a different quality.
Character turns the lights on or off.
Character draws curtains against the evening chill or opens them to let in morning sun.
The air grows cooler or hotter.

DAYS HAVE PASSED

Different weather. (For example: in the last scene, the roads were covered in snow, now the gutters are overflowing with water.)
Work has progressed. (The neighbour's garden wall is now complete).
Plants have changed. (The daffodils were budding in the previous scene, now they're in full bloom. Autumn leaves were yellowing, now they are copper-brown.)

MONTHS HAVE PASSED

Different temperature.

Drastically different weather. (Where the sun previously boiled the tarmac there's now an inch of snow.)
Seasonal changes in urban environments. (Shop windows show summer fashions in one scene and glitter with Christmas decorations in the next. Previously thriving lakeside souvenir shops are boarded up.)
Plants have changed. (Formerly verdant beech trees are now winter-bare.)

YEARS HAVE PASSED

Changes in the way buildings are used and treated. (The once-thriving neighbourhood is dilapidated, the once spotless white walls are covered in graffiti, and the once sparkling windows are smashed.)
New buildings and urban development. (The field where the cattle grazed is now a shopping centre with a parking lot. The noisy building site is now a sparkling new house.)
Changes in plants. (One scene shows rows of newly-planted saplings, the next a mature forest in the same place.)

PROFESSIONAL EXAMPLES

Autumn dwindled into early winter, with the last ploughing done and the sheep and cattle driven down from the farthest hill pastures. (Margaret Frazer: *Circle of Witches*)

By then summer was nuzzling autumn's neck. The days seemed equally long and hot, but towards dusk the air began to cool more quickly. (Lindsay Davis: *The Silver Pigs*)

Hesta had come down the garden, to the brick wall at its end. On the way, she had examined the leaning, ancient, winter-bare trees. (Tanith Lee: *When the Lights Go Out*)

By the time Dahoud reached the arena, only a glimmering thread of daylight remained. (Rayne Hall: *Storm Dancer*)

As the sun dipped below the horizon and their shadows stretched away from them, the two riders reached the edge of the plain and turned south at the base of the hills. (Nick Brown: *The Siege*)

ASSIGNMENTS

1. Compile a list of ideas how to show the passing of hours, months and years. This list will come in useful for your future works of fiction.

2. Look at the scenes of your current WiP. How much time has passed between one and the next? What change could you mention to give the reader a sense of time?

CHAPTER 21: EFFECTIVE WORD CHOICES

Specific words paint a clear picture for the reader. They make your descriptions vivid, and you convey a lot with very few words.

For example:

He walked down the tree-lined road, passing a woman with a dog in front of a building.

This creates only a vague picture of the place and is boring.

With the same or similar number of words, you can create a specific picture instead:

He ambled along the poplar-lined boulevard, passing a lady with a poodle in front of a villa.
He strode along the avenue lined with cherry trees, past a tart with a mongrel in front of a cottage.
He marched down the oak-lined cul-de-sac, passing a redhead with a Rottweiler in front of a mansion.
He hurried along the palm-lined highway, past a Goth girl with a puppy in front of a bungalow.

Use the most specific word you can think of. It will do the best job.

Here are some generic nouns to watch out for: *road, street, house, building, plant, tree, flower.* These are so vague that they need an adjective to create a picture: a small house, a tall tree. If you choose a specific noun, you may not need an adjective.

The following adjectives are too generic to create a picture in the reader's mind: *beautiful, ugly, wonderful, awful, bad, nice.*

VERBS MAKE YOUR WRITING VIVID

Setting descriptions are often sluggish or static, and they can slow the pace more than the scene requires or even halt the flow altogether. The trick to injecting life into a stagnant setting description is to use vivid verbs.

The most boring verb in the writer's toolkit is 'be' (*is, was, are, were*). Use it as little as possible. Guard especially against sentences starting with *There is/was/are/were*.

The following verbs are better, but still not great: *move, sit, stand, lie*.

Verbs are what creates your distinct author voice. Feel free to choose them creatively, and don't feel restricted by convention. Pick verbs which shows what something does.

When revising your draft, you may want to underline all verbs in your setting descriptions, and replace them with the best possible ones.

Dull|:

There was a fortress on the mountain top.

So-so:

A fortress stood on the mountaintop.
A fortress sat on the mountaintop.

Vivid:

A fortress perched on the mountaintop.
A fortress sprawled on the mountaintop.
A fortress squatted on the mountaintop.
A fortress glowered from the mountaintop.
A fortress threatened from the mountaintop.
A fortress cowered on the mountaintop.
A fortress clung to the mountaintop.
A fortress guarded the mountaintop.
A fortress protected the mountaintop.

Dull:

There was a river in the valley.
A river moved through the valley.

So-so:

A river flowed through the valley.
A river ran through the valley.

Vivid:

A river meandered through the valley
A river raced through the valley.
A river slithered through the valley.
A river snaked through the valley.
A river pushed through the valley.
A river laboured through the valley.
A river roared through the valley.

Of course, these descriptions wouldn't fit every fortress, every river or every story—but this is precisely what makes them so good.

The verb can convey not only what is there, but the PoV character's mood. Examples:

Waves roared against the pebble beach.
Waves crashed against the pebble beach.
Waves slapped against the pebble beach.
Waves rustled against the pebble beach.
Waves caressed the pebble beach.
Waves teased the pebble beach.
Waves scraped the pebble beach.
Waves drenched the pebble beach.

This technique works especially well for landscape descriptions which otherwise can feel static.

PROFESSIONAL EXAMPLES

In these sentences, professional authors have used creative verbs to bring their setting descriptions to life:

.... towering mountains, PUSHING their dark peaks against the sky (Louis L'Amour: *Crossfire Trail*)

In the summer dusk, a wild panorama of tumbling fells and peaks ROLLED AWAY and LOST ITSELF in the crimson and gold ribbons of the western sky. To the east, a black mountain OVERHUNG us, MENACING in its naked bulk. Huge, square-cut boulders LITTERED the lower slopes. (James Herriot: *All Creatures Great and Small*)

Thick ropes of runoff water SLAPPED noisily on the concrete before COURSING in swift rivulets towards drainage gates. (Kevin Hearne: *Hexed*)

*The lane SLOPED upwards, too narrow for two people to walk abreast, just a muddy track with ragged hawthorn hedges SPILLING in on both sides. (*Tana French: *The Likeness*)

Beyond the wall the country was flat on three sides—alkali dust and heat weaves SHIMMERING over stubbles of desert growth—but to the east the ground ROSE gradually, barren, pale yellow CLIMBING into deep green where pinion SPROUTED from the hillside. (Elmore Leonard: *Trouble at Rindo's Station*)

A heavy mist LAY on the dale, SWIRLING delicately round the edges of buildings and BLANKETING the river. (Elizabeth George: *A Great Deliverance*)

MISTAKES TO AVOID

Avoid overused phrases such as *snow-capped mountains, sun-drenched beach, East meets West,* and *where time stood still.*

There was/is/are/were.. is one of the dullest phrases in the writer's toolkit. Use it only if you can think of nothing better, and not more than once or twice per book.

ASSIGNMENTS

1. Go through your settings descriptions, and replace generic words with specific ones.

2. Visualise a landscape you want the reader to see, and think of verbs which will bring it to life. Write a sentence or paragraph for it.

CHAPTER 22: WRITING ABOUT REAL PLACES

Setting your story in a real location—especially one near where you live—brings big benefits.

ADVANTAGES

1. If you know the place well, the fiction oozes authenticity. Your story feels so real to the readers that they will find it easy to suspend their disbelief about other matters, such as paranormal creatures, alien invasions and unusual human behaviour.

2. You don't need to spend time and effort on inventing locations, and can put your creative efforts towards story plots and character development instead.

3. You need to do little research, because you're familiar with everything, and if there's something you don't know, you simply pop down the road, sit in a park or coffee shop with your notebook and absorb the atmosphere.

4. When it comes to marketing your book, you have a huge advantage. Normally, it's almost impossible for authors to persuade bookshops to stock their books. But if the book has a local setting, bookshops are keen to get the book, often give it a special display, and host special events such as book signings and author readings. Even shops which sell other goods often ask for the privilege of selling a book with a local setting. You may get your book sold in souvenir shops, tourist information bureaux, museums, cafés, grocers and delicatessens.

5. Local newspapers and radio stations which seldom feature books will publish articles and broadcast interviews with the author.

6. Local organisations may invite you as a guest speaker or lecturer for events and festivals.

7. Readers in that region or town are flattered and curious, so they buy the book. They enjoy recognising the featured places, and tell their friends. This word-of-mouth is the best publicity a book can get.

8. If you set book after book in this location, the setting becomes part of your author brand, and you become *the* author who writes about so-and-so county or such-and-such town. The resulting 'local celebrity' status helps sell more books. Many writers have used this approach with great success—just think of bestselling authors like Stephen White with his thrillers plots in Boulder, Colorado, Stuart McBride who places his crime fiction in Aberdeen, Scotland, and Stephen King who sets most of his novels in fictional towns in the state of Maine.

CHOICES

You have three choices:

1. Write about the place exactly as it is or was, with its streets, restaurants, public parks, and bad areas. This approach will earn you the greatest approval from the locals, and garner most free publicity and events invitations. However, it restricts what you can do with the plot.

2. Use the real town but invent a few roads, buildings and features. Or use a real region and invent a town (as Stephen King did with the fictional town of Castle Rock in the state of Maine). This option gives you a lot of fictional freedom, but reduces the local publicity value.

3. Write about the place as it never was, but might have been, or might become. This is a good option if you write Alternate History, Steampunk or Science Fiction.

MISTAKES TO AVOID

Don't assume that a place has to be unfamiliar to you to be exciting to readers.

Many newbie writers think they need to set their stories in New York. As a result, publishers receive a glut of manuscripts with a New York setting, many of them hackneyed and riddled with factual mistakes. Instead, make your fiction stand out by setting it where you live, whether that's the outskirts of Manila in the Philippines, a village in the Scottish Lowlands, or a ranch in the American Midwest. Even if your home town seems unglamorous to you, it will fascinate your readers in other parts of the world.

Don't use a generic setting that could be anywhere and as a result lacks character. Describe places which are either real, or so specific that they feel real.

If using a real location, take care that you don't accidentally libel someone. For example, if your novel features a mayor of XYZ town who takes bribes, and a head teacher of a particular school molesting children, people may think that the real mayor is corrupt. This can lead to problems for the mayor—and also for you, because he may sue you for libel.

To prevent the fictional bad character from getting confused with the real-life person, change not only the name but the age, gender, ethnicity and so on. So if the real mayor of XYZ Town is a forty-something portly black man, make the fictional corrupt counterpart a skinny white woman in her seventies.

ASSIGNMENT

Consider if the story you're writing, or future stories you have in mind, could take place in a real location near you. If yes, would you enjoy creating several books with this setting and make it part of your author brand? Would you use the real place as it is, or with fictional modifications?

CHAPTER 23: RESEARCH

The best research is your personal experience, especially if you wrote down detailed notes.

Human memory is deceptive and will often recall only broad impressions, instead of the revealing details the writer needs. Photos help, but they're purely visual, and they only record what you thought significant at the time. You probably have photos of the spectacular sunset and your lover's smile, but not the lichen on the stone slabs and the graffiti in the alleyway.

Take a notebook wherever you go, whether it's a foreign holiday or a visit to the dentist, and jot down observations— visual details, sounds, smells and everything that evokes the atmosphere of the place. Even if you don't plan to write a story set in this place, you may some years from now, and then you'll be grateful for your notes.

To research places for your current book, try to tour those places in person. If this is not possible, experience the ambience of similar places. For example, your historical novel may be set in ancient Rome. While you can't visit an authentic ancient Roman roadside tavern, you can survey a motel and motorway restaurant, and adapt your observations to suit the story.

Books, websites and DVDs are great sources of information, but don't get hung up on factual information. Sure, correct facts are important, but what you really need is atmosphere, the small details which characterise the place. Look for eyewitness reports (what did the ruins of their village look like after the earthquake? What sounds were heard on the sinking ship?) and travelogues (writers sharing their travel adventures with readers and viewers).

Old *National Geographic* magazines and DVDs are a treasure trove for writers, filled with both geographical facts and atmospheric details.

Ask other people. With the internet, it's easy to find someone who has experienced the kind of place you want to write about. However, 'normal' people may not understand what you're after, and simply assure you that a place is 'magnificent, splendid, really great' or 'horrid, disappointing, don't go there'. If possible, ask writers—they'll understand.

The internet allows you to connect with writers all over the world, via social media and online writers groups. Ask them specific questions: "Has anyone ever been in an abandoned mine shaft? Is it cold down there? What noises can be heard?" or "What's it like to be in a horse stable at night? Sounds, smells?" or "What does an approaching hurricane sound like?"

You may want to join the Writers Research Club. Membership is free. You can ask as many questions as you like about any topic which will make your story authentic. In return, you help writers who are asking about matters within your experience. Here's the link:
https://groups.yahoo.com/neo/groups/raynes_writers_rese arch

MISTAKES TO AVOID

Don't copy 'facts' from other works of fiction. Those authors may have got it wrong, and mistakes get perpetuated this way.

Don't rely on what you think a place is like. Find out how it really is.

ASSIGNMENT

1. Do desk research for a scene you're planning or revising. Browse websites with eyewitness reports or travelogues, watch YouTube videos, ask members of your online writing group or post questions at the Writers Research Club.

2. Get first-hand experience of a place you're writing about, or one of a similar nature.

CHAPTER 24: BUILD A SETTING DESCRIPTIONS BANK

When you write a scene, you won't always have access to the real thing for an authentic experience. You may have to write about a snow storm while you sit in sweltering heat, or you may write in a mountain cabin and need to write about an inner city tenement. It may be late evening and you want to describe a village stirring to life at dawn.

In such situations it helps if you have a collection of setting descriptions. Build a Setting Descriptions Bank from which you can draw any phrases you need.

Jot down notes of all kinds of places and weather. You can do this when you have time to kill—during a long train journey, in a boring meeting, or while waiting at the dentist's. Keep a notebook with you wherever you go.

Whenever you visit a place you haven't been before, use it as an opportunity to add to your Setting Descriptions Bank: during your summer holidays in a foreign country, when you spend the weekend with your sister, or on a business trip. This will yield a rich harvest of different places.

Your own home town or village can also provide a lot of material, especially if you use it as the setting for your fiction (see Chapter 22). Even if you don't set a story there, you can observe different seasons, times of the day and weather conditions.

You can jot down whatever comes to your attention, but a systematic approach yields most results. Here's a worksheet I've created so I won't forget the most useful details. Feel free to use it as it is, or to adapt and expand it for your needs.

You may want to save it on your tablet or keep a printout in your notebook. If you need a printable doc file, email me at rayne_hall_author@yahoo.com.

WORKSHEET

1. General impressions of the place.

2. What noises are in this place? Try to find at least four. More are better. Describe each, using verbs. Listen especially to background noises; these characterise the place.

3. Two or more smells. Just list them; no need for description.

4. A small visual detail which most people would overlook but which is somehow characteristic of the place.

5. A signpost, notice, advertising poster, framed picture, announcement or warning sign (or several).

6. A brief description of the floor, ground or carpet.

7. A brief creative description of the ceiling or sky.

8. What's the weather like? How does it feel on the skin?

9. The source and quality of the light (where does the light come from? How bright is it, what colour?) Aim to convey the mood/atmosphere of the place. If appropriate, also include a sentence in which the light gives a clue to the time of the day.

10. Something incongruous—something which seems out of place.

11. If appropriate, describe a person who is part of the setting (an attendant or customer, perhaps). How is s/he dressed? How does s/he move? Watch especially the posture, the facial expression and repeated movements.

12. If people are present, overheard snippets of conversation—just brief phrases.

13. The colours of two things, creatively described.

14. One or several similes, comparing something in this place to something outside the place. For example '... looks like...', '...sounds like...', '....smells like....', '... as big as...', '... as if....', '... slower than....', '...reminds me of...'

15. A door. What does the door look like? How does it sound when it opens? How does it sound when it closes?

16. A plant. (Flowers drooping in a vase? Brambles overgrowing the garden? Tulips standing like soldiers in orderly rows? A shrub clinging to the cliff face?)

17. An animal. (Dead fly on the windowsill? Fat spider dangling from the ceiling? Owl hooting in the distance? Fat sheep grazing in the valley? Dogs chasing one another?)

18. Touch. How something feels when you touch it with your hand. (e.g. is the doorknob cold, warm, rough, smooth, sticky?)

19. Taste. Describe how something tastes—but only if it's relevant to the setting, for example, when describing a pub or coffee shop.

20. Anything else.

EXAMPLES FROM RAYNE'S SETTINGS DESCRIPTION BANK

Living on the south coast of England, I have collected lots of descriptions related to the seashore in every season and weather, including this one in October:

The sea is low churning brownish grey topped with sheets of dirty froth. In the distance, it looks blue-grey ruffled and streaked. During recent stormy nights, the sea has thrown stones (rust, grey, near white) up on the promenade, as well as driftwood (mostly fibrous, with all colour leached out) some charred branches, twigs, short frayed pieces of neon-green nylon rope and tangles of black bladderwrack. This debris lies mostly near the top of the beach. Large bird feathers stick like bedraggled trophies or markers out of the stones.

This is the same stretch of beach in August:

After weeks of cold weather, everyone comes out to grab the sunshine. Londoners pour from their city down to the coast, crowding beach. They stream along every path and road, carrying baskets and carrier bags and life preservers and iceboxes and heavy parasol stands. Their boomboxes thump out grating rhythms; apparently these people cannot bear the majestic silence of the sea, with its soft-rustling waves and seagull chatter. They wear wearing shorts and bare-shouldered dresses, platform-heeled flip-flops in dark shades or sequinned flip-flops revealing lacquered toes.

The wind tugs at my hair and shirt. White shells dot the sand. The sand under my bare soles is hard-ridged, damp, solid, but when I reach the water's edge, it feels velvety soft. The water is cool as it sloshes around my ankles. The tide is low. Small foam-crested waves glide towards me with faint rustling sounds, one after the other, and caress my ankles.

These are my notes from a run-down internet café:

The computer makes a constant scratching sound like fingernails running across a chalkboard. The mouse and keyboard feel sticky to the touch. On the wall, pin-up photos of young girls in uncomfortable poses, splotches of Blu-tack and drawing pins. The chairs run on castors; their lower parts are black, scuffed and thick with dust.

The grey carpet with small red and yellowish-grey pattern. It's sprinkled with crumbs and dark splotches, mended with broad blue sticky tape that curls up at the corner. Some customers' blank shoes look shiny against the dull dusty carpet.

When I visited a historic prison, now turned into a museum, I took these notes about what it's like inside a cell:

The cell's just wide enough to lie down and stand up in. The walls and ceilings are mostly brick but with some timber. Timbers are carved with prisoners' graffiti, including 'Thomas Hall was put in jail December 1822'. The floor looks like concrete, mottled and cracked. A small window, recessed, squarish, with two vertical and two horizontal bars, opens into the corridor. Since the corridor has no roof, some daylight enters through this window. A wooden bed bench along the wall is topped with a metal sheet which feels cold to the touch. A straw-filled hessian sack serves as a mattress. In a corner stands a metal bucket. The door—black on the outside, grey on the inside—moves noiselessly. At about the height of my throat, there's a square flap opening outwards, presumably for the prisoners' food. The flap squeaks when I open it; its knob rattles.

I have thousands of setting descriptions, and I refer to them frequently. Whatever I need, I probably have something—if not exactly right, then similar enough to adapt. My only regret is that I did not collect detailed setting descriptions years ago when I lived and travelled in China, Mongolia, Tunisia and Greece.

ASSIGNMENT

Walk down the road where you live, and answer the questions in the worksheet.

SAMPLE STORY

Here's one of my short stories, illustrating how I use setting descriptions in my fiction.

DOUBLE RAINBOWS

Gerard hurried down the spiral staircase of Sibyl's lighthouse, his shoes clanking on the metal steps. The blue steel hands of his Rolex showed 8.13. The tide had turned two hours ago, and he did not want to get his new boots wet as he hiked home.

The steep chalk path from the promontory to the seabed was slippery with smudge from the night's rain. The sea surface glinted like a diamond-sprinkled sheet, and the air smelled of salty seaweed. In the distance, gulls cackled and squealed.

His chest brimmed with pride at how well he had handled the situation. Breaking to your girlfriend that you would marry someone else required a delicate touch, especially if she was pregnant. At first, she had hurled reprimands. Then she had demanded that he leave her home. But the high tide already submerged the way out, and she had to let him stay the night.

After a lot of coaxing and consoling, her rants subsided to sobs. Gently, he pointed out that as an artist, she was above conventions like monogamy and marriage, and that single motherhood was all the rage. When he assured her she would remain the love of his life, and promised to continue his Friday night visits, she had stared at him in wide-eyed wonder. By morning, she had clung to him with surprising passion.

Sibyl had amazing curves, flaming hair and a temper to match, vivid imagination but little practical sense. She refused to sell the dilapidated lighthouse to one of the wealthy buyers queuing for 'converted character properties', insisting she loved living surrounded by sea. Isolated when the tide rose twice a day, with only her paintings for company, she lived for Gerard's weekly visits.

Driftwood, whelk eggs and cuttlefish bones littered the low-tide seabed, and bundles of dark bladderwrack lay entangled like scorched spaghetti. As he skirted around chunky boulders, the smell of fishy seaweed grew stronger, wavering between fresh and foul.

Rust-brown shingle and splinters of flint crunched under his fast steps. He had three miles to cover before the incoming tide wet his feet.

In the east, the sun was already painting the sky a brisk blue, but in the north, a curtain of silver-grey rain still veiled the view. A rainbow beyond the promontory framed the lighthouse in bright glory. He squinted. Was that a second rainbow emerging inside the large one? Even as he looked, the faint hues strengthened. Two rainbows, two women—the perfect omen for his fortunate future. Sibyl had probably spotted it already. He pictured her standing at the large window in her round room, paintbrush in hand, plotting to shape the vision into a painting.

But Gerard had no time to linger and watch the rainbows grow, because the tide waited for no man. Everything about nature—the sun, the rain, the rainbows, the tides—followed complex rhythms, regular but never the same. All was calculable—he patted the tide table in his jeans pocket—yet never quite as expected. Atmospheric pressure, moon phases and such all played a role. Stirred by wind and swelled by the rain, today's sea was already higher than normal.

Waves swished and slurped and rustled across the shingle. He took firm, even steps past black rocks, across broken shells and white crab corpses. Water ran in thin streams between sand and stones, down the almost unnoticeable slope towards the sea.

Soon he would have both: a rich wife and an unconventional mistress. A fair man, he would give both women the attention they deserved, but this required skilful planning. Erica could not be relied upon to show the same flexibility as Sibyl; she might even expect to have her husband to herself. He had to show tact and not spoil her illusions. A job involving absences from home would help, preferably no longer in her father's employ.

At 8.22, he reached the mainland shore where cliffs towered like steep castle walls. Thirteen feet above, sparse grasses grew in cracks, and gorse shrubs clung to precarious holds. Below that, nothing found a grip on the stark rock face, nothing survived the high tide.

He had another hour and a quarter to walk on the seabed to the end of the cliff that lined the shore. The wind rose, whipped up waves and sculpted them into mountain ridges. Puddles filled, and water streamed into rock pools. With the hem of his shirt, he wiped the thin coating of salt from his spectacles, and squinted at the sea. The tide was coming faster than it should.

An illusion, no doubt, from a water level raised by wind and rain. Today's high tide was at 13.01, which meant the sea did not hit the cliff until 10.30, and then he would be past the inaccessible part and on dry secure land.

He checked his watch again, just in case. The blue steel hands on the silvered dial showed 8.28 as it should. A quick glance back revealed the bill already washed by water, the route he had walked submerged by the incoming tide. Only its tip, the rock with the lighthouse, still pointed like an admonishing finger out of the sea. The rainbow was now clearly a double, its colours sharp.

Ignoring natural laws, the water crawled closer, brushing the scattered rocks with angry lashes and frothy caress. Puddles filled and forced Gerard to take big strides from rock to rock.

He checked the tide table, ran his finger down the column for today's high tide. 13.01. He was right, and had an hour and a half to clear the rest of the cliff.

Was the sun supposed to stand so high at half past eight? All he knew was that it rose from the east. On previous walks, he had not paid it much attention. He always left Sibyl's place at low tide, which was a different time every week, so the sun was never in the same place anyway. Though the sun looked high, and the water was close.

What if his watch had stopped? A Swiss Rolex was supposed to be infallible. *Ticke-tac, ticke-tac, ticke-tac,* the watch assured him, and the minute hand moved another notch.

As the water's edge sneaked nearer, he scanned the cliff face for an escape. Surely there was some gap, some path, some stairs hewn into the rock? But he had walked this route on many Saturday mornings, and knew there was none. Thoughts and fears whirled through his mind, questions, worries and doubts.

A drop of sweat slid down his back, and another. Keeping close to the cliff, he marched faster.

Wall-like waves crashed and shoved sheets of white foam at his feet. Tendrils of panic curled into his stomach while gulls glided past in mocking calm.

A cloud blocked out the sun. The air chilled and pimpled the skin on his arms, even as the sweat of fear pasted the shirt to his back. To his left, the cliff stood smooth, steep, merciless.

Salty splashes stained his shoes, sneaked into his socks, soaked his trouser legs. The drum of fear beat in his chest. With the watch pressed to his ear, he ran.

Boom boom boom, his heart thudded. The watch went *ticke-tac, ticke-tac, ticke-tac* above the hiss of the waves.

The water rose fast. Icy wet snaked around his ankles, his calves. Still the cliff stretched without end.

No one could have reset the watch except last night.

Sweet Sybil. So grateful, so forgiving.

The next wave slammed his chest against the rock with ice-cold force.

FURTHER READING

If you want to delve deeper into the pleasures of setting descriptions, here are some great books to explore.

Rebecca McClanhan: *Word Painting—A Guide to Writing More Descriptively*. This book inspires creative descriptions, not just for settings.

Jack M. Bickham: *Setting—How to Create and Sustain a Sharp Sense of Time and Place in Your Fiction*. This guide shows how to weave plot, characterisation and setting together.

Mary Buckham: *Active Setting*. This is a four-book series delving deep into the craft of bringing settings to life. Volume 1: *Characterization and Sensory Detail*. Volume 2: *Emotion, Conflict and Back Story*. Volume 3: *Anchoring and Action*. Volume 4: *Hooks*.

DEAR READER,

I hope you enjoyed this book and have discovered many ideas how to make your setting descriptions vivid and compelling.

Email me how you got on with this book and which chapters have been most useful to you, and also if you spotted any typos which have escaped the proofreader's eagle eyes. My email address is: **rayne_hall_author@yahoo.com.** You can also contact me on Twitter: @raynehall.

If you find this book helpful, it would be great if you could spread the word about it. Maybe you know other writers who would benefit.

Reviews on sites like Amazon, Barnes & Noble, GoodReads, BookLikes etc. are very welcome. Email me the link to your review, and I'll send you a free review copy (ebook) of one of my other Writer's Craft books. Let me know which one you would like: *Writing Fight Scenes, Writing Scary Scenes, The Word-Loss Diet, Writing About Magic, Writing About Villains, Writing Dark Stories, Writing Short Stories to Promote Your Novels, Twitter for Writers, Why Does My Book Not Sell? 20 Simple Fixes.*

You may want to take a peek at a sample chapter of *The Word-Loss Diet* at the end of this book.

With best wishes for writing success,

Rayne Hall

SAMPLE: THE WORD-LOSS DIET

Welcome to Dr. Rayne's Word-Loss Diet. If your writing needs toning up or slimming down, you've come to the right place.

I'll show you how to shed thousands of words from your overweight manuscript without changing the plot.

I'm uniquely qualified to write this book, because I used to be the wordiest writer ever. I tended to use fifty words where five would do, and rejection letters from editors contained comments like 'wordy', 'needs tightening', and 'not fast-paced enough for us'.

At first, I huffed: how dare this editor suggest that anything in my precious prose could be cut! My stories needed those words!

However, I was also an editor, and I found it easy to spot superfluous words in other writers' wordy wafflings. Eventually I applied the same techniques to my own prose. I learnt to revise my wordy drafts so they became tight, often with less than half the wordage of the original. To my surprise, the tighter versions were really better.

In this book I'll share my most effective slimming tricks. It took me two decades to learn them. You'll master them in a few days.

The book is based on my online class The Word-Loss Diet. Students who completed the class shed five, ten, even twenty percent of their words, and their writing style became leaner and stronger. Many students say the class was the best investment they ever made. Now you can study the same programme in book form, at your own pace.

You can apply all the techniques to give your manuscript a complete stylistic makeover—this will take between five and fifty hours—or you may apply only some techniques to address problem areas. The choice is yours.

This book is perfect for polishing a manuscript before submitting to agents or before indie publishing. It can also help if you need to trim an over-long manuscript to meet wordcount requirements, or if you're wondering why your writing keeps getting rejected.

Before you start working with this book, prepare yourself for some shocking insights. Almost everyone gets an 'Ouch!' reaction when they discover weaknesses in their writing style. You may cringe with embarrassment when you realise those flaws.

Not everyone is ready for this kind of insight. If you're a novice writer just starting out, this book may be discouraging. If you're feeling low, my advice may be too harsh, and the insights may shatter your confidence. Put the book aside for now and pick it up again when you're ready.

If you're confident in your writing and keen to improve it further, if you're ready to take your writing skills to the next level and don't mind some 'Ouch!' experiences, then this book is for you. We will strip the layers of fat from your writing and expose the muscle of your unique author voice.

With every technique in this book, you choose whether you want to apply it and to what extent. You're the CEO of your writing; I'm only the consultant. You decide which words to keep and which to discard.

If you're used to American English, some British words, spellings and grammatical constructions may look odd, but I'm sure you will understand me anyway.

Now brace yourself and transform your waffling writing into tight, exciting prose. Are you ready?

LET'S START TO BEGIN

Here are two phrases you can cut without loss:

* begin to (begins to, beginning to, began to, begun to)

* start to (starts to, starting to, started to)

If something happens, you don't need to tell the reader that it starts to happen. Just let it happen.

Examples:

Obese
She began to run.
Slim
She ran.

Obese
Rain began to fall.
Slim
Rain fell.

Obese
She started to shiver.
Slim
She shivered.

Obese
His lips started to quiver.
Slim
His lips quivered.

Obese
The dog started to growl.
Slim

The dog growled.

BEGINNER WEAKNESS

The unnecessary use of 'begin to' and 'start to' is the sign of a novice writer. Editors who see them on the first page know the submission comes from a novice. This may not be the kind of signal you want to send.

Consider removing all 'begin to' and 'start to' from the sample chapters before you submit them.

EXCEPTIONS

Should you avoid 'start to' and 'begin to' altogether?

Not necessarily. Sometimes, when an action starts and is abandoned immediately, they help clarify what's going on:

She began to walk home, but changed her mind after a few steps.

He started to paint the fence, but Jane halted his arm.

ASSIGNMENTS

1. Use the 'Find&Replace' function (explained in the Introduction) to highlight 'start', 'begin', 'began', 'begun' with a red background. Depending on the text-processing software you use, the steps are something like this:

* Open a manuscript. I suggest using a copy, so you don't spoil the real one if things go wrong.

* Choose the word you want to highlight. For example, 'start'.

* Click 'Edit'.

* A drop-down menu appears. Click 'Find&Replace'.

* In the 'Search for' box, type 'look'. In the 'Replace with' box, also type 'start'.

* Move the cursor into the 'Replace with' box and click there.

* Click 'More options'.

* A drop-down menu appears. Click 'Format'.

* Click 'Background'.

* A window appears with many little coloured squares. Click a bright colour, for example, green.

* Click 'ok'

* Now you're back to the 'Find&Replace' window. Click 'Replace all'.

* The programme highlights every single 'look' in your manuscript in green. You can see at a glance if you've overused the word and where. It also says 'search key replaced 1025 times' or however many times you've used the word, which may be more often than you thought.

Try it. Once you got the hang of it, it's quick.

Caution: some programmes don't differentiate between upper and lower case, which can lead to 'Start' being replaced with 'start'. The search will also bring up other words containing that string, for example 'startling'.

Sit back and assess your manuscript on the screen. Does it look like a rash of green measles? Congratulations: you've discovered an easy way to improve your writing style and shed a lot of words.

2. Take a note of the manuscript's current wordcount. Then kill as many 'start to' and 'begin to' as possible. Compare the 'before' and 'after' wordcount. How many words have you shed today? Can you see the how your style has improved?

66960900R00062

Made in the USA
Charleston, SC
01 February 2017